An Analysis of

Alexander Hamilton, James Madison, and John Jay's

The Federalist Papers

T0349553

Jeremy Kleidosty
with
Jason Xidias

www.macat.com
info@macat.com

Cover illustration: Capucine Deslouis

Cataloguing in Publication Data
A catalogue record for this book is available from the British Library.
Library of Congress Cataloguing-in-Publication Data is available upon request.

ISBN 978-1-912303-27-4 (hardback)
ISBN 978-1-912127-63-4 (paperback)
ISBN 978-1-912282-15-9 (e-book)

Notice
The information in this book is designed to orientate readers of the work under analysis,
to elucidate and contextualise its key ideas and themes, and to aid in the development
of critical thinking skills. It is not meant to be used, nor should it be used, as a
substitute for original thinking or in place of original writing or research. References and
notes are provided for informational purposes and their presence does not constitute
endorsement of the information or opinions therein. This book is presented solely for
educational purposes. It is sold on the understanding that the publisher is not engaged
to provide any scholarly advice. The publisher has made every effort to ensure that
this book is accurate and up-to-date, but makes no warranties or representations with
regard to the completeness or reliability of the information it contains. The information
and the opinions provided herein are not guaranteed or warranted to produce particular
results and may not be suitable for students of every ability. The publisher shall not be
liable for any loss, damage or disruption arising from any errors or omissions, or from
the use of this book, including, but not limited to, special, incidental, consequential or
other damages caused, or alleged to have been caused, directly or indirectly, by the
information contained within.

CONTENTS

THE MACAT LIBRARY

The Macat Library is a series of unique academic explorations of seminal works in the humanities and social sciences – books and papers that have had a significant and widely recognised impact on their disciplines. It has been created to serve as much more than just a summary of what lies between the covers of a great book. It illuminates and explores the influences on, ideas of, and impact of that book. Our goal is to offer a learning resource that encourages critical thinking and fosters a better, deeper understanding of important ideas.

Each publication is divided into three Sections: Influences, Ideas, and Impact. Each Section has four Modules. These explore every important facet of the work, and the responses to it.

This Section-Module structure makes a Macat Library book easy to use, but it has another important feature. Because each Macat book is written to the same format, it is possible (and encouraged!) to cross-reference multiple Macat books along the same lines of inquiry or research. This allows the reader to open up interesting interdisciplinary pathways.

To further aid your reading, lists of glossary terms and people mentioned are included at the end of this book (these are indicated by an asterisk [*] throughout) – as well as a list of works cited.

Macat has worked with the University of Cambridge to identify the elements of critical thinking and understand the ways in which six different skills combine to enable effective thinking.
Three allow us to fully understand a problem; three more give us the tools to solve it. Together, these six skills make up the **PACIER** model of critical thinking. They are:

ANALYSIS – understanding how an argument is built
EVALUATION – exploring the strengths and weaknesses of an argument
INTERPRETATION – understanding issues of meaning

CREATIVE THINKING – coming up with new ideas and fresh connections
PROBLEM-SOLVING – producing strong solutions
REASONING – creating strong arguments

To find out more, visit **WWW.MACAT.COM.**

CRITICAL THINKING AND *THE AGE OF REVOLUTION*

Primary critical thinking skill: REASONING
Secondary critical thinking skill: EVALUATION

The 85 essays that maker up *The Federalist Papers'* clearly demonstrate the vital importance of the art of persuasion. Written between 1787 and 1788 by three of the "Founding Fathers" of the United States, the Papers were written with the specific intention of convincing Americans that it was in their interest to back the creation of a strong national government, enshrined in a constitution – and they played a major role in deciding the debate between proponents of a federal state, with its government based on central institutions housed in a single capital, and the supporters of states' rights.

The papers' authors – Alexander Hamilton, James Madison, and John Jay – believed that centralised government was the only way to knit their newborn country together, while still preserving individual liberties. Closely involved with the politics of the time, they saw a real danger of America splintering, to the detriment of all its citizens.

Given the fierce debates of the time, however, Hamilton, Jay and Madison knew they had to persuade the general public by advancing clear, well-structured arguments – and by systematically engaging with opposing points of view. By enshrining checks and balances in a constitution designed to protect individual liberties, they argued, fears that central government would oppress the newly free people of America would be allayed.

The constitution that the three men helped forge governs the US to this day, and it remains the oldest written constitution, still in force, anywhere in the world.

ABOUT THE AUTHORS OF THE ORIGINAL WORK

Alexander Hamilton (1755 or 1757–1804) was born in the British West Indies. An aide to George Washington during the American Revolution, he went on to establish the US Department of the Treasury.

James Madison (1751–1836) was born into a wealthy plantation-owning family in Virginia; he later wrote the first draft of the US Constitution and became the fourth president of the United States.

John Jay (1745–1829) was born in New York City. A lawyer and politician, he was the first chief justice of the US Supreme Court. They are considered three of America's "Founding Fathers."

ABOUT THE AUTHORS OF THE ANALYSIS

Dr Jeremy Kleidosty received his PhD in international relations from the University of St Andrews. He is currently a postdoctoral fellow at the University of Jväskylä, and is the author of The Concert of Civilizations: The Common Roots of Western and Islamic Constitutionalism.

Dr Jason Xidias holds a PhD in European Politics from King's College London, where he completed a comparative dissertation on immigration and citizenship in Britain and France. He was also a Visiting Fellow in European Politics at the University of California, Berkeley. Currently, he is Lecturer in Political Science at New York University.

ABOUT MACAT

GREAT WORKS FOR CRITICAL THINKING

Macat is focused on making the ideas of the world's great thinkers accessible and comprehensible to everybody, everywhere, in ways that promote the development of enhanced critical thinking skills.

It works with leading academics from the world's top universities to produce new analyses that focus on the ideas and the impact of the most influential works ever written across a wide variety of academic disciplines. Each of the works that sit at the heart of its growing library is an enduring example of great thinking. But by setting them in context – and looking at the influences that shaped their authors, as well as the responses they provoked – Macat encourages readers to look at these classics and game-changers with fresh eyes. Readers learn to think, engage and challenge their ideas, rather than simply accepting them.

'Macat offers an amazing first-of-its-kind tool for interdisciplinary learning and research. Its focus on works that transformed their disciplines and its rigorous approach, drawing on the world's leading experts and educational institutions, opens up a world-class education to anyone.'

Andreas Schleicher,
Director for Education and Skills, Organisation for Economic Co-operation and Development

'Macat is taking on some of the major challenges in university education ... They have drawn together a strong team of active academics who are producing teaching materials that are novel in the breadth of their approach.'

Prof Lord Broers,
former Vice-Chancellor of the University of Cambridge

'The Macat vision is exceptionally exciting. It focuses upon new modes of learning which analyse and explain seminal texts which have profoundly influenced world thinking and so social and economic development. It promotes the kind of critical thinking which is essential for any society and economy. This is the learning of the future.'

Rt Hon Charles Clarke, former UK Secretary of State for Education

'The Macat analyses provide immediate access to the critical conversation surrounding the books that have shaped their respective discipline, which will make them an invaluable resource to all of those, students and teachers, working in the field.'

Professor William Tronzo, University of California at San Diego

WAYS IN TO THE TEXT

KEY POINTS

- Alexander Hamilton, James Madison, and John Jay wrote the 85 essays that make up *The Federalist Papers*. They were published in 1787 and 1788.

- Written under the pseudonym Publius,* *The Federalist Papers* were in favor of the ratification (or approval) of a new US Constitution* so that the United States would have a stronger political union, a more robust economy, and the ability to fend off foreign aggression.

- Along with the Declaration of Independence* and the US Constitution, *The Federalist Papers* are founding documents of the United States. They have served as a basis for American government and law, and as a reference point for wider debates on democracy* and human rights.*

Who were Alexander Hamilton, James Madison, and John Jay?
Alexander Hamilton was the first secretary of the United States Treasury,* John Jay was the first chief justice of the US Supreme Court,* and James Madison later became fourth president of the United States (1809–17). Hamilton and Madison were delegates at the Constitutional Convention,* which drafted the new Constitution in 1787.

These three important figures wrote *The Federalist Papers* under the pseudonym Publius, a reference to an ancient Roman politician who overthrew the monarchy in favor of a Roman republic. Hamilton, Madison, and Jay applied their knowledge of political philosophy alongside the political needs of late eighteenth-century America to advocate a Constitution that would ensure the stability and well-being of the United States. Today, these three figures are regarded as being among the country's Founding Fathers.*

The authorship of some of the papers is disputed. According to American historian Douglass Adair,* Hamilton conceived the project and wrote papers 1, 6–9, 11–13, 15–17, 21–36, 59–61, and 65–85; Madison wrote papers 10, 14, 37–58, and 62–3; Hamilton and Madison cowrote papers 18–20; and John Jay wrote papers 2–5 and 64. While Hamilton produced more content than Madison, and Madison more than Jay, the contributions of all three were significant. Madison's views were particularly influential as he had drafted much of the Constitution.[1]

What Does *The Federalist Papers* Say?

The Federalist Papers are a collection of 85 essays, published in eighteenth-century New York, that together argue for a strong and active central government. A new US Constitution had been presented by a Constitutional Convention to the 13 individual states for ratification. *The Federalist Papers* argue in favor of ratification and against the status quo under the existing Articles of Confederation.* Two of the authors of *The Federalist Papers*—Hamilton and Madison— were delegates at the Convention.

The Articles of Confederation, which effectively formed the first Constitution of the United States, had been ratified in 1781 and provided for a loose confederation (alliance) of self-governing states and a weak national legislature (the body that passes laws). That arrangement was designed explicitly in opposition to the strong central government of Great Britain, and in the context of the War of Independence from Britain that took place between 1775 and 1783. The newly independent United States of America therefore had a natural suspicion of centralized government. In some ways it would seem logical for there to be natural hostility toward a new Constitution that looked to put more power into the hands of a single central power.

From the perspective of the authors of *The Federalist Papers*, however, the Articles of Confederation had failed to achieve political and economic security and would likely fail to hold the union together. The essays drew on European Enlightenment* and republican* philosophy in considering which form of government most effectively balanced individual rights and the broader interests of society. The Enlightenment was a seventeenth- and eighteenth-century movement that emphasized progress through science and reason. Republican philosophy was in favor of government that represented the rights and needs of the public. It was argued by some that the American political experiment under the Articles of Confederation had proved that too much liberty meant that an orderly and prosperous society could not exist. The authors tried to show how the United States could both retain state autonomy and still protect personal liberty through strong government.

These themes are reflected in the titles of some of the papers:
- "The Insufficiency of the Present Confederation to Preserve the Union"
- "Advantage of the Union in Respect to Economy in Government"
- "Concerning Dangers from Foreign Force and Influence"
- "Concerning Dangers from Dissensions Between the States"
- "Concerning the General Power of Taxation"

It is not agreed whether the essays directly influenced the ratification of the new Constitution. While their initial aim was to persuade the state of New York to ratify, that state did not, in fact, do so until after nine other states had ratified. At least nine states needed to ratify before the Constitution could be passed into law. But even so, it is clear that the authors saw their vision realized. The new Constitution provided for a stronger federal* government—that is, one in which power is shared between local and national layers of government through defined institutions—with a chief executive (president), courts, and powers of taxation.

Why Does *The Federalist Papers* Matter?

Along with the Declaration of Independence and the US Constitution, *The Federalist Papers* form one of the founding documents of the American republic. Hamilton, Madison, and Jay wrote them in a unified voice for a specific purpose—to increase public support for the new US Constitution. Anti-Federalists*—those who didn't agree with the idea of a government where power is shared between local and national layers—saw the Constitution as a threat to state powers and individual freedoms. In defending their cause, the three authors made persuasive arguments rooted in the ideas of classical and modern political philosophers. They also reflected the anxieties and concerns of the young nation. The 85 essays gave impetus to the constitutional project, but they have also had an enduring effect as a foundation for American government and law, as well as having broader influences on debates on democracy—a system of government in which the people exercise power, either directly or through elected representatives—and human rights—the basic rights and freedoms to which all people are entitled.

The Federalist Papers are a landmark statement of American political philosophy and are still relevant beyond the US. Just as the Americans of the 1780s grappled with the balance between liberty and order, and with the relationship of people to their governments, countries today have different ways of addressing that balance between freedom and the need for security. In addressing the spectrum between centralized and decentralized governments, *The Federalist Papers* are also relevant to present-day separatist movements*—where one group wishes to break away from another—worldwide. American judges have used *The Federalist Papers* to help them interpret the Constitution and, by the year 2000, they had been quoted 291 times in Supreme Court decisions.[2]

NOTES

1   Douglass Adair, "The Authorship of the Disputed Federalist Papers," *William and Mary Quarterly* 1, no. 2 (1944): 97–122; Douglass Adair, "The Tenth Federalist Revisited," *William and Mary Quarterly* 8, no. 1 (1951): 48–67.

2   Ron Chernow, *Alexander Hamilton* (New York: Penguin, 2004), 260.

SECTION 1
INFLUENCES

MODULE 1
THE AUTHOR AND THE HISTORICAL CONTEXT

KEY POINTS

- *The Federalist Papers* show how people can work together to produce a coherent political philosophy. They provided a foundation for American government and law.

- The writers—Hamilton, Madison, and Jay—had diverse family backgrounds, but all three were trained in classical and modern political philosophy.

- The core message in the 85 essays is that a stronger central government and legal system are necessary to ensure the survival of America and the well-being of its people.

Why Read this Text?

The Federalist Papers are a collection of essays published in New York between October 1787 and August 1788. Written by three important political figures in the country's early history, they were designed to persuade fellow countrymen to accept a new set of supreme laws, the Constitution.* These authors—Alexander Hamilton, James Madison, and John Jay—were convinced that the existing Constitution (the Articles of Confederation*) was no longer fit for purpose.

The authors were already important national figures. James Madison had penned the first draft of the Constitution himself. Alexander Hamilton had been an aide to future President George Washington* during the American Revolution/War of Independence* (1775–83) and went on to establish the Department of the Treasury.* John Jay had worked as both a politician and a

> 66 The Founding Fathers conducted intense studies of political history to help them found the new federal and state governments. They studied great political thinkers including Aristotle, Cicero, Cato, Hume, Montesquieu, and Locke, along with the classical histories of Plutarch, Livy, and Tacitus. 99
>
> Donald Lutz,* *A Preface to American Political Theory*

diplomat, and had founded the country's judicial (court) system. As such, all three can claim to be "Founding Fathers"* of the United States.

The Federalist Papers are hugely interesting historically, but they are also fascinating because of their literary techniques of persuasion. They have played a central role in helping people understand American legal and constitutional issues and the relationship between efficient government and economic stability,[2] and in debates on democratization*—the process of making countries more democratic—and human rights.*

The Federalist Papers offer a sophisticated take on the principles of good governance. The newspaper publication of these articles, from late 1787 to summer 1788, had a significant impact on American political and legal opinion at the time. Subsequent book editions aroused great interest as well.

The essays argued for a number of political principles:

- Republicanism,* a system in which the people are sovereign (the ultimate power) and government acts on their behalf.
- Federalism,* a system in which sovereignty (lawmaking power) is shared between different levels of government.
- Separation of powers,* the division of powers between the executive (administrative), the legislative (lawmaking), and the

judicial (court) branches of government. This separation is designed to create a check on executive power.

The fundamental principles of *The Federalist Papers* are also adaptable: they are referred to today in political and legal battles over international trade and Internet privacy.[3] *The Federalist Papers* are a seminal text in political science, law, history, and philosophy.

Author's Life

Alexander Hamilton was born in the British West Indies (the British Empire territories in the Caribbean), the son of an absent merchant father and a shopkeeper mother. There is debate about his birth date, but he himself thought it was 1757. He was effectively orphaned at the age of 12 when his mother died of fever. Hamilton had already gained a reputation as a writer when, in 1772, at the age of 15, he left to complete his education in America with funds donated by fellow islanders. He first studied at Elizabethtown Academy in New Jersey and then at King's College in New York (now Columbia University).

James Madison was born into a wealthy, slave-owning plantation family in Virginia in 1751 and studied at the College of New Jersey (now Princeton University). One of his teachers was John Witherspoon,* a specialist in the works of the Scottish Enlightenment,* a period in the eighteenth century when huge leaps in intellectual and scientific thinking took place. These ideas on political and economic freedoms influenced the American Revolutionary movement of 1775 to 1783 that led to the country's independence from Britain.

John Jay was born in 1745 to a wealthy New York City family of merchants and government officials. He was educated as a lawyer at King's College before establishing a law practice and becoming engaged in politics.

Despite these different family histories and personal circumstances, all three men shared a good education and an understanding of classical and modern political philosophy.

Some scholars have argued that the writers' family backgrounds explain their individual political leanings. As the son of a merchant family with ties to Scottish aristocracy, Hamilton is often portrayed as pro-business and pro-elite.[4] In contrast, Madison's family was involved in state government, which may have influenced his views on states' rights.* John Jay's preference for social order probably reflects his family's legal background and his upbringing in the established Anglican Church.*[5]

Author's Background

The Articles of Confederation were the first Constitution of the United States. They were drawn up during the War of Independence and had been in effect since 1781. But it had quickly become clear that the Articles were unable to satisfy all the needs of the 13 states of the Union. In February 1787, delegates from the states met in Philadelphia to revise the Articles of Confederation at the Constitutional Convention.*

The new Constitution that arose from this meeting was in favor of a stronger national government and fewer powers for the individual states. It proposed a national executive with a president and the power to tax. To some, this seemed precisely the centralized power that the Thirteen Colonies*—the colonies that formed the original United States—had opposed when they fought the British. Those opposed to the new proposals became known as Anti-Federalists.* Those in favor of the new Constitution were Federalists.* It was against this backdrop that the authors wrote *The Federalist Papers*.

Both Hamilton and Madison had already argued for stronger central government and had asked for more funding for Congress*— the existing federal government of the country—during the late 1770s and early 1780s.[6] But the idea of linking together a better-funded and more sophisticated government took shape only in *The Federalist Papers* and in the drafting of the new Constitution itself.

NOTES

1   Donald Lutz, *A Preface to American Political Theory* (Lawrence: University Press of Kansas, 1992), 136–8.

2   A few examples of these uses include Keith Whittington, *Constitutional Interpretation: Textual Meaning, Original Intent, and Judicial Review* (Lawrence: University Press of Kansas, 1999); Bernard Grofman and Donald A. Wittman, *The Federalist Papers and the New Institutionalism*, Series on Representation (New York: Agathon Press, 1989); David Held, "Democracy: From City-States to a Cosmopolitan Order?", *Political Studies* 40 (1992): 10–39; Michael Meyerson, *Liberty's Blueprint: How Madison and Hamilton Wrote the Federalist Papers, Defined the Constitution, and Made Democracy Safe for the World* (New York: Basic Books, 2008).

3   See Kyle Scott, *The Federalist Papers: A Reader's Guide* (New York: Bloomsbury Academic Publishing, 2012), 173. Also George H. Carr, "Application of US Supreme Court Doctrine to Anonymity in the Networld," *Cleveland State Law Review* 44 (1996): 521; Grofman and Wittman, *The Federalist Papers and the New Institutionalism*.

4   See, for example, Lawrence S. Kaplan, *Alexander Hamilton: Ambivalent Anglophile*, Biographies in American Foreign Policy Series (Wilmington: SR Books, 2002), 3–20.

5   Walter Stahr, *John Jay: Founding Father* (New York and London: Hambledon, 2005), 4–14.

6   For calls in the pre-Constitutional era for a stronger US government, see E. James Ferguson, "The Nationalists of 1781–1783 and the Economic Interpretation of the Constitution," *Journal of American History* 56, no. 2 (1969): 241–61.

MODULE 2
ACADEMIC CONTEXT

KEY POINTS

- Hamilton, Madison, and Jay were looking to create a stronger political union with a new Constitution.* They believed that this would ensure economic prosperity, defense against aggression, and well-being for the American people.

- The authors believed that the federal* government should have sufficient power to represent and protect the interests of the people, but that a separation of powers* was necessary to avoid corruption and abuse.

- The authors applied classical and modern political philosophy to the uncertain and unstable American context of the late eighteenth century to back up their arguments.

The Work In Its Context

The intellectual environment of late eighteenth-century America was steeped in Greek and Roman classical works and the Enlightenment.* The Enlightenment emphasis on rationality, progress through cooperation, and individual liberty and tolerance was fundamental to the values that the American founders wanted to express through their system of government. As the United States was a relatively new country, intellectual debates often had a direct impact on political decisions because there had been no previous models on which decisions could be based.

In September 1787, the new Constitution of the United States was presented to all of the states for ratification. Anti-Federalists* published articles in the New York press in an effort to defeat it, claiming it would lead to the oppression of state interests and of individual liberties.

> ❝ What is government itself but the greatest of all reflections on human nature? If men were angels, no government would be necessary. If angels were to govern men, neither external nor internal controls on government would be necessary. In framing a government which is to be administered by men over men, the great difficulty lies in this: you must first enable the government to control the governed; and in the next place, oblige it to control itself. ❞
>
> James Madison, "Federalist No. 51"

Under the alias Publius, the Federalists* struck back, carefully responding to each Anti-Federalist concern. Alexander Hamilton, John Jay, and James Madison, the authors of *The Federalist Papers*, argued that a new Constitution would ensure a strong and efficient federal government, consolidate an American national identity, and ensure internal stability and a formidable defense against foreign aggression. These articles helped persuade those originally against the Constitution in New York and other states to support the initiative.

Overview of the Field

The classical theme that power corrupts and must be limited is found throughout *The Federalist Papers*. Likewise, the Enlightenment belief that government should be representative of the people and should provide a system in which education and industry can flourish is present in almost all of the essays. These ideas not only influenced the authors, they also served as an important way to support their positions. They were meant to appeal to similarly educated people who would find such historical references more persuasive than arguments made by their contemporaries.

Through references to philosophy and the existing political

system, the writers were proposing a novel way of combining strong national government with a high degree of personal liberty. The balancing of political institutions, the justification for restraining the power of different social groups, and the emphasis on a good government's potential to enhance personal freedom were highly original.

Academic Influences

The name "Publius" reveals a great deal about the authors' inspirations. Though from extremely different family backgrounds, the authors were all educated at elite schools and were well versed in the Greek and Roman classics. They read great thinkers such as Aristotle,* Cicero,* Plutarch,* Thomas Hobbes,* and John Locke.*

Human behavior had always been studied by classical and modern scholars. For example, in *Politics*, Aristotle argued that "man is by nature a political animal,"[1] and in *Leviathan*, Hobbes suggested that in the absence of a strong government, society would be a "war of all against all."[2] Agreement about how much human nature was predetermined or timeless, however, was challenged by many other thinkers. These included David Hume,* who suggested that human nature reflected physical aspects that could exert an influence, and Immanuel Kant,* who thought that human society could achieve progress—and that human nature could therefore be improved—through education.

The influence of these thinkers and others is acknowledged throughout the text. The authors of *The Federalist Papers* agreed with Aristotle that human nature needed governing, but also applied Kant to call for progress and peace.[3] In "Federalist No. 14" Madison discusses democracy* and republicanism* with reference to ancient Greece. The ancient Greeks considered democracy the worst form of government because it could turn into mob rule and chaos. So Madison highlighted a difference between modern republicanism— equally concerned with protecting the rights of minorities as with representing majorities—from the democracy of the ancient world.[4]

NOTES

1 Aristotle, *The Politics*, trans. Carnes Lord (Chicago: The University of Chicago Press, 1984), 37.

2 Thomas Hobbes, *Leviathan* (London: Hackett, 1994), Chapter XIII, Section 9.

3 Alexander Hamilton et al., *The Federalist Papers*, ed. Isaac Kramnick (Harmondsworth: Penguin, 1987), 318–20.

4 Richard M. Gummere, "The Classical Ancestry of the United States Constitution," *American Quarterly* 14, no. 1 (1962): 13–14. Also Hamilton et al., *The Federalist Papers*, 141.

MODULE 3
THE PROBLEM

KEY POINTS

- When *The Federalist Papers* were published, the key question being debated was: how can the United States defend its territory, while improving the stability of its political institutions and the welfare of its people?

- The main participants in this debate were the Federalists,* who were in favor of the ratification of a new Constitution,* and the Anti-Federalists*, who wanted to keep the existing Articles of Confederation.*

- The Federalist authors defended their position by using persuasive arguments rooted in classical and modern philosophy.

Core Question

The core question addressed by Alexander Hamilton, James Madison, and John Jay, the authors of *The Federalist Papers*, was: how can the United States preserve its territorial integrity and defensive capability while at the same time improving the stability of its political institutions and promoting the general welfare of its people? As "Federalist No. 23" states, "The principal purposes to be answered by Union are these—the common defense of the members—the preservation of the public peace as well against internal convulsions as external attacks—the regulation of commerce with other nations and between the States—the superintendence of our intercourse, political and commercial, with foreign countries."[1]

These themes were central to the questions of whether a new Constitution was necessary and whether the document being debated was the ideal instrument for achieving the aims outlined above. The

> **❝ After an unequivocal experience of the inefficacy of the subsisting federal government, you are called upon to deliberate on a new Constitution for the United States of America. ❞**
> Alexander Hamilton, "Federalist No. 1"

Federalists believed that the Articles of Confederation had failed. While the Articles protected state interests against a powerful federal government, they had not managed to stop tensions rising between the states, nor prevent an unwillingness to pay taxes to the federal government. Frustrated by the fact that Congress* was almost powerless to enforce the laws it passed, the Federalists promoted the passing of a new Constitution. They argued that it would encourage an American national identity.

The Participants

Through *The Federalist Papers*, Hamilton, Madison, and Jay wanted to show how the US government would work under a new Constitution. To do so, they discussed human nature, republicanism,* federalism,* and the nature of political unions. They made strategic use of ancient and modern political philosophy and applied those ideas to the contemporary political context. By doing this they made the arguments they presented to the American public more credible.

Most Federalists were wealthy, well educated, and interested in orderly government that could protect their status. They were well organized and used their influence in the approval process. Anti-Federalists were generally farmers and workers who were loyal to their state governments. Their leaders included Patrick Henry* and George Mason,* who argued that a centralized government would lead to tyranny.

The publication of the essays in New York newspapers not only meant that they were quickly distributed and widely read, it also invited public debate and responses from critics such as the Anti-Federalists, who attempted to argue that state governments should hold the majority of political power. Although Anti-Federalists were especially strong in the states of New York, Virginia, and Rhode Island, they ultimately lost out to the force and sophistication of the Federalist arguments.

The Contemporary Debate

Classical political thought revolved around how the state could develop "the good life" for its citizens. Inquiries tend first to define what "the good life" actually means in social terms and then outline a plan to achieve it. The writers of *The Federalist Papers* were conscious of being part of a long-standing philosophical tradition. But they also thought they were doing something novel, adapting the ideals of philosophy to the practicalities of political negotiation and the specific problems created by the democratic* ideals of the new state. Chief among these was the dilemma of how to respect the principle of majority rule* (the principle that whatever a majority of citizens decide with regard to a voting issue should become law), while still ensuring that fundamental rights were respected for *all* citizens, especially ethnic and religious minorities.[2] The idea that minorities can easily be persecuted in a democratic regime was crucial to their understanding of the purposes of government. And this influenced the writers' decision to focus on limiting government power through a system of checks and balances.

The authors approach these questions in a number of ways. In several of the essays they quote extensively from influential Greek, Roman, French, and English thinkers, including Cicero,* Montesquieu,* and John Locke.* The authors make use of historical references too. They talk about Athens and Rome, as well as about more recent political experiences in Great Britain and post-

Independence America. This impressive philosophical and historical knowledge was then used to propose a stronger Constitution for the United States and to outline how the new document corrected existing problems with the Articles of Confederation.[3]

NOTES

1 Alexander Hamilton et al., *The Federalist Papers*, ed. Isaac Kramnick (Harmondsworth: Penguin, 1987), 184.

2 Todd Donovan and Shaun Bowler, "Direct Democracy and Minority Rights: An Extension," *American Journal of Political Science* 42, no. 3 (1998): 1020–1.

3 Kyle Scott, *The Federalist Papers: A Reader's Guide* (New York: Bloomsbury Academic, 2012), 3–7.

MODULE 4
THE AUTHOR'S CONTRIBUTION

KEY POINTS

- *The Federalist Papers* were written to encourage support for the ratification of the new US Constitution,* but also to offer practical explanations as to how this new form of government would work.

- A new Constitution went far beyond simply revising the Articles of Confederation.* Giving the federal government greater power was controversial, because America had just gained independence from a highly centralized Britain.

- The authors united the ideas of great classical and modern political philosophers with contemporary debates in America to make a persuasive argument in favor of a new Constitution.

Author's Aims

The authors of *The Federalist Papers*—Alexander Hamilton, James Madison, and John Jay—wanted radical political change. Facing the prospect of a ratification vote for the new US Constitution, they intended to use their essays to generate support for the pro-ratification cause. But *The Federalist Papers* are more than political propaganda or persuasion. They also act as a blueprint for government: how the new institutions will work, how they will interact, and how they will respond to society at large. In explaining the issues of how the Constitution would actually work and the political theory behind it, the authors seized more opportunities to persuade people that their plans were sound. They also responded to Anti-Federalist* fears

> 66 The opinions expressed by the authors of that work [*The Federalist Papers*] have been justly supposed to be entitled to great respect in expounding the Constitution. No tribute can be paid to them which exceeds their merit; but in applying their opinions to the cases which may arise in the progress of our government, a right to judge of their correctness must be retained. 99
>
> John Marshall, former chief justice of the US Supreme Court

regarding how people in "big" government could abuse their power and how this type of government might overstretch itself.

The Federalist Papers make clear that the US has a unique opportunity to make decisions at an early stage in its political development. Either the states could support a strong Constitution and the future of America or they could accept the status quo. In the view of Hamilton, Madison, and Jay this meant instability, both internally and against the prospect of an external threat.

Approach
Each author of *The Federalist Papers* contributed in the areas of his expertise: stronger government for Hamilton, government institutions for Madison, and foreign policy for Jay.

Scholars such as Kyle Scott* say that the work is best approached in four sections:
- "Federalist Nos. 1–14" stress the importance of political union in securing political stability.
- "Federalist Nos. 15–22" point out the shortcomings of the Articles of Confederation.
- "Federalist Nos. 23–36" suggest that these problems can be fixed through stronger and more active federal* government.

- "Federalist Nos. 37–85" outline:
- how government departments will function
- how this will make the government effective and able to protect the rights and liberties of citizens
- how the proposed system is a practical application of philosophical ideals of political freedom and public well-being.[2]

The first essays detail how the new union will benefit the state of New York and the entire United States. They then show how the new Constitution is a superior form of government compared to the existing Articles of Confederation. Next, they explain the new institutions and the ideas behind their creation. They then conclude with a discussion of how the new Constitution will protects rights despite not having a Bill of Rights* specifically to do that. There were also reminders of the contents of the other essays.[3] This is an effective rhetorical* strategy: identify a problem, outline a solution, show how the solution is superior to the status quo, and finally remind the audience of their role and stake in the outcome.

Contribution In Context

The authors of *The Federalist Papers* helped to bring about a better understanding of the US Constitution. Reading the Constitution itself does not explain how the checks and balances between the different branches of government prevent any one of them from becoming too powerful. But "Federalist Nos. 47–51" address the separation of powers* (dividing the role of lawmaking from the role of law enforcement) both in depth and with great nuance. The issue of tyranny (or abuse of power) was also implicit in discussions of how minority rights could be protected through representative government. Madison used "Federalist No. 10" to show that the causes of political factions or groups cannot be eradicated. Their effects, however, can be alleviated by enlarging the scope of the state to encompass a diversity of interest groups. This means that every faction has a reasonable expectation of political success, but none feels entitled to it.

Beyond the value of explaining the Constitution to those voting either to ratify or to deny its passage, *The Federalist Papers* have played a crucial role in court judgments and continue to do so. Scholars such as Pamela Corley,* Robert Howard,* and David Nixon* point out that the essays are used to interpret the Constitution and play a key role in helping Supreme Court* justices persuade their colleagues in writing court opinions.[4]

NOTES

1   Walter Malins Rose, *United States Supreme Court Reports* (Michigan: The Lawyers Cooperative Publishing, 1901), 431.

2   Kyle Scott, *The Federalist Papers: A Reader's Guide* (New York: Bloomsbury Academic Publishing, 2012), 49.

3   Scott, *The Federalist Papers*, 3–7.

4   Pamela C. Corley et al., "The Supreme Court and Opinion Content: The Use of the Federalist Papers," *Political Research Quarterly* 58, no. 2 (2005): 329–40.

SECTION 2
IDEAS

MODULE 5
MAIN IDEAS

KEY POINTS

- The key themes of *The Federalist Papers* are: the shortcomings of the Articles of Confederation,* the need for a stronger federal* government, the importance of political union, and how government should function.

- The text argues that a stronger central government was more than a philosophical ideal—it gave the United States the best chance of survival.

- The authors persuasively responded to the criticisms of the Anti-Federalists* in their 85 essays.

Key Themes

The Federalists were in favor of a new Constitution because, in their view, the Articles of Confederation had failed. The federal government was too weak. States had been given excessive power during the struggle against a centralized Britain and because of a fear of a "tyranny of the majority."* This latter phrase summed up the fear that in a democracy* the majority view would simply drown out minority voices that actually needed to be heard. Under the Articles of Confederation, Congress* had no power to impose taxes, it could not draft troops for war, it could not control interstate commerce, states printed their own money, and the US government had no chief executive to enforce the laws it passed. The Federalists advocated stronger central government in response to this, and in order to forge a national identity.

Alexander Hamilton, James Madison, and John Jay's *The Federalist Papers* proposed transferring certain specified powers, such as coining

> ❝ It has been frequently remarked, that it seems to have been reserved to the people of this country, by their conduct and example, to decide the important question, whether societies of men are really capable or not, of establishing good government from reflection and choice, or whether they are forever destined to depend, for their political constitutions, on accident and force. ❞
>
> Alexander Hamilton, "Federalist No. 1"

money and declaring war, from individual states to the central government. The central authority would be divided into three branches of government—the legislative (lawmaking), executive (putting laws into effect), and judicial (court) wings—and two houses of Congress—the Senate* and the House of Representatives.* A system of checks and balances between these branches and houses would safeguard against abuses of power. It was also proposed that states would retain full control over all areas not reserved for the central authority. There would, in addition, be some shared powers such as taxation and the courts.

The benefits of political union form a core idea. In "Federalist No. 14," Madison writes, "We have seen the necessity of the Union, as our bulwark against foreign danger, as the conservator of peace among ourselves, as the guardian of our commerce and other common interests, as the only substitute for those military establishments which have subverted the liberties of the Old World, and as the proper antidote for the diseases of faction, which have proved fatal to other popular governments, and of which alarming symptoms have been betrayed by our own."[1] Political union, therefore, was part of the project to forge a common American identity.

The papers attempted to achieve a balance between the views of Hamilton, who reflected the commercial interests of New York, and the views of Madison, who understood the concerns of Virginia farmers about a powerful distant authority. Together, they believed they could express a vision for a cohesive nation without destroying the identity or autonomy of all the states.

Exploring The Ideas

The intellectual debate in eighteenth-century America was both political and philosophical. Competing interests had a stake in the outcome, including state legislators, judges, political parties, citizens, and businesses. *The Federalist Papers* are recognized as key writings on good governance and its intellectual foundations. But they represented only some of the competing interests of the day.

Anti-Federalists used arguments from America's "Founding Fathers,"* such as James Wilson.* Wilson argued that a government relying on the consent of the people to be legitimate needed its citizens to obey laws of their own free will and for them to have a natural attachment to the state. Anti-Federalists claimed that there therefore needed to be smaller local governments with which people could identify more easily.[2]

"Federalist No. 9" challenges this argument. Hamilton notes that his opponents cite Montesquieu* (a French Enlightenment* lawyer) when arguing for small republics. But Hamilton points out that most of the 13 states were already bigger than what Montesquieu recommended. Hamilton also suggests that the Anti-Federalist reading of Montesquieu was both selective and misleading. He quotes Montesquieu at length to show that he had, in fact, advocated a "confederacy"—"a convention by which several smaller states agree to become members of a larger one ... A republic of this kind, able to withstand an external force, may support itself without any internal corruptions."[3]

Other schools of thought were part of both Federalist and Anti-Federalist circles. Political conservatism* had a role in opposing the new US Constitution. Although conservatives acknowledged the benefits of a broader American identity and better military defense, they were skeptical that the Constitution was the way to achieve both.

The Federalist Papers should be read as an explanation of the Constitution, an argument for its adoption, and a response to Anti-Federalist opposition to it.[4]

Language And Expression

The Federalist Papers are both foreign and familiar to modern readers. The lyricism of the language, the sentence structure, and the references to classical literature make it clear that they are historical documents. The constitutional language used may be complex for nonspecialists. However, the discussions on why governments are needed and the relative merits of different forms of government are current and timeless.

Some editions of *The Federalist Papers* change the prose to make them more accessible to a wider readership. Words such as "visionary" or "fabulous," which today usually have positive meanings, are edited to "impractical" or "foolish" to convey their original meanings.[5] The original text has a great deal of beauty, though, and some may dislike this kind of tinkering.

Yet others, such as Kyle Scott,* a political scientist and author of a reader's guide to *The Federalist Papers*, find the full collection to be "disorderly" and in need of an external guide: "It does follow an order, but it can go off track at times, which can make the order appear unclear and leave the reader trying in vain to tie up the loose ends. Its sheer size makes a reader's guide helpful."[6]

NOTES

1   Alexander Hamilton et al., *The Federalist Papers*, ed. Isaac Kramnick (Harmondsworth: Penguin, 1987), 140–1.

2   Herbert J. Storing, *The Complete Anti-Federalist* (Chicago: The University of Chicago Press, 2008), 1: 15–17.

3   Hamilton, "Federalist No. 9."

4   For an interesting discussion of the current relevance of Anti-Federalist ideas, see Carol M. Rose, "The Ancient Constitution vs. the Federalist Empire: Antifederalism from the Attack on Monarchism to Modern Localism," *Northwestern University Law Review* 84, no. 3 (1989): 74–105.

5   See, for example, Hamilton et al., *The Federalist: With Letters of "Brutus"*, ed. Terence Ball (Cambridge: Cambridge University Press, 2003), xlvii.

6   Kyle Scott, *The Federalist Papers: A Reader's Guide* (New York: Bloomsbury Academic Publishing, 2012), 45.

MODULE 6
SECONDARY IDEAS

KEY POINTS

* Important secondary themes in the text include: human nature, the separation of powers,* and why factions spring up.

* The authors combined these elements into a comprehensive argument showing how a new Constitution* would ensure good governance, unity, and prosperity.

* These secondary ideas have been cited in a range of debates, including discussions on the tension between individual freedoms and the need for social order.

Other Ideas

There are a large number of secondary ideas in *The Federalist Papers*. Among the most important are ideas and thoughts about human nature, political union, the distribution of wealth, republicanism,* and federalism.*

Although the authors, Alexander Hamilton, James Madison, and John Jay, wanted above all to convince fellow citizens to support the US Constitution, other ideas are brought in to support that aim. Some touch on why people need government and how a government can best match the social and psychological states of humankind.

Madison's view of human nature is an important secondary theme because it helps to explain why he believed a new Constitution was necessary. The United States was an overwhelmingly Protestant* nation with a rather pessimistic view of the human tendency to sin. Madison believed that strong republican government could control

> **❝** The latent causes of faction are thus sown in the nature of man ... [A]n attachment to different leaders ambitiously contending for pre-eminence and power; or to persons of other descriptions whose fortunes have been interesting to the human passions, have ... divided mankind into parties ... and rendered them much more disposed to vex and oppress each other than to co-operate for their common good ... But the most common and durable source of factions has been the various and unequal distribution of property. **❞**
>
> James Madison, "Federalist No. 10"

such imperfections.

In "Federalist No. 51," Madison argues for a separation of powers—a system of checks and balances between the legislative (lawmaking), executive (putting laws into effect), and judicial (court) branches of government, and between the two houses of Congress;* that is, the Senate* and House of Representatives.* He believes that this system will help avoid a "tyranny of the majority."*

Madison also notes in "Federalist No. 10" the tendency for people to form factions, or interest groups. This he sees as potentially contrary to the common good. While Madison acknowledges a number of ways in which this might come about, he sees the unequal distribution of property as a fundamental cause. He was not opposed to such inequality, but proposed that a republican form of government based on elected representatives would ease its worst effects.

Exploring The Ideas

The secondary ideas appear throughout the text and could be characterized as a political framework for the new Constitution. The question of human nature is evident in "Federalist No. 51:" "If angels were to govern men, neither external nor internal controls on government would be necessary. In framing a government which is to be administered by men over men, the great difficulty lies in this: you must first enable the government to control the governed; and in the next place oblige it to control itself."[1]

Here Madison links human nature to the need for the Constitution and at the same time notes why governments need to be governed themselves. This continues to be relevant today in considering the behavior of government and the balancing of individual freedoms against social justice.

Unequal distribution of property wealth as a cause of division could easily be seen as an argument for a more equal distribution and so a more just society. But Madison was clear at the end of "Federalist No. 10" that an equal division of property would be an "improper or wicked project." His purpose in this case is to argue for a "republican remedy" to such problems.

Overlooked

Because of its status as a key piece of American political writing, there can be little in *The Federalist Papers* that has escaped examination. A suggested area for further exploration was the Anti-Federalist* response to the ideas in *The Federalist Papers*.[2] Debates cannot be fully appreciated when one side is less well known. The Anti-Federalist side is not likely to attain the status of *The Federalist Papers*, but there has been much scholarly work on the Anti-Federalists. As such, it can no longer be considered an overlooked area of research.[3]

Economics and business interests in relation to the national government are frequently discussed in *The Federalist Papers*. When the United States was founded it was a preindustrial state with limited international trade and commerce. Today it is the world's largest economy, with a massive international footprint. The essays dealing with taxation, with the allocation of financial powers to either state or national bodies, and with regulations for interstate commerce and trade treaties are therefore far more relevant today than they were at the time when they were written.

This has made *The Federalist Papers* more relevant in studies of political economy* and economics generally. Their interpretation of trade law has also been researched, and the text is now instrumental in regulating American trade relationships in a way consistent with the country's wider constitutional values.[4]

NOTES

1 Alexander Hamilton et al., *The Federalist Papers*, ed. Isaac Kramnick (Harmondsworth: Penguin, 1987), 319–20.

2 See William Jeffrey Jr., "The Letters of 'Brutus': A Neglected Element in the Ratification Campaign of 1787–88," *University of Cincinnati Law Review* 40 (1971): 643.

3 Hamilton et al., *The Federalist Papers*, 82.

4 For an example of this type of work, see Bernard Grofman and Donald A. Wittman, *The Federalist Papers and the New Institutionalism*, Series on Representation (New York: Agathon Press, 1989).

MODULE 7
ACHIEVEMENT

KEY POINTS

- The arguments of *The Federalist Papers* helped in the ratification of the US Constitution.*

- Despite strong opposition, all 13 states eventually adopted it.

- The authors published their essays in a particular American context. However, many of their points about government, law, and individual rights are relevant to other contexts.

Assessing The Argument

Alexander Hamilton, James Madison, and John Jay's *The Federalist Papers* helped to ensure that the Constitution was ratified. Despite strong opposition, Virginia (which included what is now West Virginia and Kentucky) and New York became the 10th and 11th states to adopt the new Constitution, in large part because of the influence of Alexander Hamilton and John Jay themselves.[1] Although only nine states were required for formal ratification, having these two populated and economically important states on board was seen as essential for the country's political cohesion.

The Federalist Papers are counted among the classics of political thought in various anthologies and are cited in numerous cases in the US Supreme Court.* They continue to hold a central place in debates about the proper role of government in democratic* countries.[2] There has been an active debate over the lasting legacy of the work, and whether it actually reflects a proper understanding of the US Constitution. But even its critics acknowledge that it was a fundamentally important work in its own time and that it continues to

> **❝** The great accomplishment of *The Federalist Papers* was to show that the Constitution was both coherent and republican … By drawing out the reasoning latent in the text and completing it with his reasoning, Publius presented the Constitution as an achievement in good government—a plan not only worthy of momentary applause but of the rational and enduring consent of an enlightened public. **❞**
>
> Charles R. Kessler, "Introduction," *The Federalist Papers*

inspire discussion and study today.[3]

Achievement In Context

The core ideas of *The Federalist Papers* reflect the preoccupations of the early American republic, including the way people thought about state sovereignty,* the use of government power, and the proper role of a national government in the future United States. Anti-Federalists* were mainly determined to ensure their rights were not eroded and that democratic participation did not disintegrate because of a more powerful ruling elite. Madison and Hamilton in particular strove to calm these fears. Madison was keen to introduce another issue for consideration: minority rights. He felt it was crucial to show that democratic governance had to include limitations on government powers to ensure that the rights of different groups could not be eroded through legislation.[4]

The main intended audience for these essays was twofold. The most immediate audience was the public of New York State. The essays were, after all, published in local newspapers and were meant for circulation. The fact that the essays were quickly collated into a two-volume work and then published suggests they were also supposed to be read by a national audience. While Hamilton felt the work was meant to make a timeless case,[5] Madison took it to be a manifesto for a specific time and place: the "authentic exposition of the text of the Federal Constitution."[6]

Limitations

The Federalist Papers form a work that Hamilton, Madison, and Jay intended for multiple audiences and purposes. This is reflected in statements from the two men who wrote the great majority of the text. Alexander Hamilton, who conceived the project and wrote 60 percent of it, was known for his confidence and desire for greatness. It is unsurprising that he claimed that the authors looked "forward to remote futurity"—or what would happen in the future.[7] On the other hand, Madison really did cement his own legacy by drafting the Constitution and serving as president. He wrote in 1825 that the book is "the most authentic exposition of the text of the Federal Constitution, as understood by the Body which accepted it."[8] This was meant to show that the work was primarily suited to understanding the Constitution in its original context, which narrows its applicability in other situations. Both authors were right, however, in that the text served its immediate purpose well and still continues to be relevant in the "remote futurity."

The role of *The Federalist Papers* in American jurisprudence (the science or philosophy of law) is established. But the US Constitution's status as the oldest written Constitution still in force, and the fact that it served as an inspiration for subsequent democratic constitutions, means that *The Federalist Papers* are relevant to non-American contexts as well.[9] They are also important in areas that are not purely political or philosophical, and are cited in economics,[10] rhetoric,*[11] and other fields.

Most of the text has been criticized in a way that is specific to North American political culture, but it has also been used in Latin American and other contexts, meaning that its application has extended beyond simply "remote futurity" to remote localities too.[12]

NOTES

1   Alexander Hamilton et al., *The Federalist Papers*, ed. Isaac Kramnick (Harmondsworth: Penguin, 1987), 38.

2   Hamilton et al., *The Federalist Papers*, ed. Clinton Rossiter (Harmondsworth: Penguin, 2003), 11–12.

3   See an interesting portrait of how different scholars assess its influence in Michael Meyerson, *Liberty's Blueprint: How Madison and Hamilton Wrote the Federalist Papers, Defined the Constitution, and Made Democracy Safe for the World* (New York: Basic Books, 2008), 135–44.

4   Gordon S. Wood, "Ideology and the Origins of Liberal America," *William and Mary Quarterly* 44, no. 3 (1987): 630–2.

5   Hamilton et al., *The Federalist Papers*, 76–81.

6   Hamilton et al., *The Federalist Papers*, 76–81.

7   Hamilton et al., *The Federalist Papers*, 80.

8   Hamilton et al., *The Federalist Papers*, 81.

9   David Held, "Democracy: From City-States to a Cosmopolitan Order?", *Political Studies* 40 (1992): 10–39.

10 Bernard Grofman and Donald A. Wittman, *The Federalist Papers and the New Institutionalism*, Series on Representation (New York: Agathon Press, 1989).

11 James Jasinski, "Heteroglossia, Polyphony, and the Federalist Papers," *Rhetoric Society Quarterly* 27, no. 1 (1997): 23–46.

12 Deborah J. Yashar, "Democracy, Indigenous Movements, and the Postliberal Challenge in Latin America," *World Politics* 52, no. 1 (1999): 76–104.

MODULE 8
PLACE IN THE AUTHOR'S WORK

KEY POINTS

- The authors' entire outputs focused on improving governance and law to ensure political and economic stability and general welfare.

- Although *The Federalist Papers* drew from earlier writings by Hamilton and Madison, they were the high points of their intellectual careers.

- *The Federalist Papers* are founding documents of the American nation and continue to have a major influence today.

Positioning

Published under the pseudonym Publius, Alexander Hamilton, James Madison, and John Jay's *The Federalist Papers* are a multi-authored work that cannot be placed in a single author's corpus. Hamilton wrote the majority of the essays, followed by Madison and then Jay.[1] But by considering the careers of all three, it is possible to see where their respective essays fit into the overall body of their own writing.

For Hamilton and Jay, *The Federalist Papers* represented the height of their intellectual contributions to political theory and society. Both wrote a number of documents in their positions as, respectively, first US Treasury* secretary and US Supreme Court* justice, but *The Federalist Papers* are unique for addressing good governance in the context of an entire political system rather than relating to specific problems and remedies.

Madison perhaps gained the most from the success of *The Federalist Papers*. He was respected for having drafted much of the Constitution

> **❝** Among the numerous advantages promised by a well-constructed union, none deserves to be more accurately developed, than its tendency to break and control the violence of faction. **❞**
> James Madison, "Federalist No. 10"

and understood its content as well as anyone. He later became secretary of state and president, positions he held for a total of 16 years. Today, Madison is widely regarded as the father of the US Constitution.

Integration

The role of *The Federalist Papers* in the implementation and interpretation of the US Constitution has surely contributed to their success and longevity. Each of the authors had the opportunity to experience the actual operation of their political theory by holding different major leadership roles in the US federal government: Madison as president, and Hamilton and Jay in their aforementioned posts. Based on their letters and speeches in later years, the authors seem to have mostly remained firm in their views of how the institutions and the relationships between them should function. However, they did differ on the applicability of the text and its legacy, with Madison alone seeming to feel it was primarily a document of its own time, useful for understanding the US Constitution in its historical context.

Madison wrote a number of essays in 1791 and 1792 critiquing the political theory of the French lawyer and thinker Montesquieu,* even though they shared a belief in the doctrine of the separation of powers.* These essays developed ideas first expressed in the US Constitution and *The Federalist Papers*.[2] Hamilton seems to have been consistent in his own views and referred back to his work when making later decisions while in office.[3] Madison and Hamilton were professional politicians as well as theorists, so examples of inconsistency in their decisions and their writings do exist. These, however, may best be put down to the need for political compromise rather than a fundamental change of mind.

Significance

The Federalist Papers are a classic of political theory. The arguments made by Hamilton, Madison, and Jay echoed earlier philosophical debates about the organization of government and society. This is not just a text relevant to the late eighteenth century, but is, rather, a seminal source of information. It has been an important point of reference for political scientists and has been immensely influential as a way of interpreting the US Constitution for every branch of the American government. Indeed, it has achieved an almost legal status in jurisprudence (or legal theory). In short, *The Federalist Papers* have served as a guidebook on how government and law should work and are today cherished as one of the founding documents of the United States.

The Federalist Papers have also shaped debates in other parts of the world on issues such as democracy,* individual rights, minority rights, republicanism,* popular sovereignty, political union, and the separation of powers.[4] The European Union,* for example, is a system of governance that is sometimes loosely compared with the form of government in the United States.

NOTES

1 Douglass Adair, "The Authorship of the Disputed Federalist Papers," *William and Mary Quarterly* 1, no. 2 (1944): 97–122; Douglass Adair, "The Tenth Federalist Revisited," *William and Mary Quarterly* 8, no. 1 (1951): 48–67.

2 Colleen A. Sheehan, "Madison and the French Enlightenment: The Authority of Public Opinion," *William and Mary Quarterly* 59, no. 4 (2002): 925–7.

3 Michael Meyerson, *Liberty's Blueprint: How Madison and Hamilton Wrote the Federalist Papers, Defined the Constitution, and Made Democracy Safe for the World* (New York: Basic Books, 2008), 135–62.

4 Guillermo O'Donnell, "Horizontal Accountability in New Democracies," in *The Self-Restraining State: Power and Accountability in New Democracies*, ed. Andreas Schedler et al. (Boulder, CO: Lynne Rienner Publishers, 1999), 146–7.

SECTION 3
IMPACT

MODULE 9
THE FIRST RESPONSES

KEY POINTS

- Anti-Federalists* forcefully opposed the establishment of a new Constitution.*

- Publius* published 85 essays between 1787 and 1788 that persuasively responded to criticisms from Anti-Federalists.

- Important factors that shaped the positive reaction to *The Federalist Papers* were the weaknesses of the Articles of Confederation* and the authors' convincing arguments.

Criticism

Alexander Hamilton, James Madison, and John Jay were aware that *The Federalist Papers* would attract a great deal of criticism. The essays took an open position in favor of adopting the new US Constitution and made no attempt to be objective. The authors were trying to persuade skeptical voters that adopting the Constitution was the best possible thing to do. They took the Federalist* title for their position and forced the opposition to become the Anti-Federalists (in spite of the pseudonym used in the quote above). In other words, this work was designed to attract and encourage critical debate. The entire text has been scrutinized in detail by political philosophers, judges, and citizens ever since.

Anti-Federalists argued that *The Federalist Papers* made an unconvincing case for constitutional ratification. They thought that questions on the relationship between state and national governments were left unanswered and made light of real threats to personal and political liberties.

Anti-Federalists also adopted pseudonyms in the fashion of the day.

> **❝** Those furious zealots who are for cramming it down the throats of the people, without allowing them either time or opportunity to scan or weigh it in the balance of their understandings, bear the same marks in their features as those who have been long wishing to erect an aristocracy. [1] **❞**
>
> A Federalist, *The Anti-Federalist Papers, No. 1*

One Anti-Federalist calling himself "Cincinnatus" (after a Roman aristocrat) criticized the Federalist argument for a unified and strong central government on the ground that American colonial and Revolutionary experience showed that small, local government was the best system for ensuring freedom. He asked his readers, "Will anyone believe … that in twelve years we are to overthrow every system which reason and experience taught us right?"[2] Anti-Federalists like Cincinnatus rejected the idea that the Articles of Confederation were not working and argued that, on the contrary, they were performing just as they were supposed to by keeping government small and local.

Responses

The three authors responded to Anti-Federalist arguments on an ongoing basis. Each time an essay was published in a newspaper, it attracted public comment and letters to the editor, and was often mentioned in an opponent's response. Subsequent essays could therefore respond to critiques directly, making *The Federalist Papers* part of a political dialogue in which the reader could get a feel for both sides of the debate by reading just the one.

Indeed, Anti-Federalist arguments were occasionally rejected explicitly. This is seen in the title of "Federalist No. 39": "The Conformity of the Plan [Constitution] to Republican Principles: An

Objection in Respect to the Powers of the Convention Examined." This essay acknowledged the Anti-Federalist claim that the Constitutional Convention* (which met to revise the Articles of Confederation) was illegitimate because it went beyond what it was authorized to do.[3] The Anti-Federalist fear was that centralized government would simply end up disregarding state power. Madison's response was that the Senate* would reflect state interests and that the national government's power would extend "to certain enumerated objects only, and [leave] to the several States a residuary and inviolable sovereignty over all other objects."[4] Any power that was not specified as belonging to the center would automatically fall to the states.

While the authors did not give ground on the fundamental issues at stake, they did tailor their arguments to respond to the concerns of both critics and the wider voting public. The Anti-Federalists ultimately had trouble responding to the volume of Federalist arguments.

Conflict And Consensus

The Anti-Federalists did not win the constitutional debate but they still left an important legacy. In the period leading up to the ratification of the Constitution, the Anti-Federalists had argued that the separation of powers that the Federalists wanted was not enough to prevent government tyranny. Once the new Congress* was convened, states such as Massachusetts demanded further assurances. Out of this came a series of amendments to the new Constitution and the first 10 amendments became a new Bill of Rights.*

The key criticisms raised by the Anti-Federalists—the dangers of big government, the need to respect majority rule* more than minority rights, the rejection of the idea that political loyalty should rest primarily with the national government rather than with the governments of the individual states[5]—have remained fully part of American politics ever since, for instance with regard to slavery, the discriminatory Jim Crow laws,* suspicion of federal power in

Washington, and a wide array of other issues.

Despite this tension, *The Federalist Papers* showed how the American experiment in combining federalism and republicanism* could work.[6] They are recognized as key founding documents of the United States.

NOTES

1 Written by "A Federalist" (anonymous), "A dangerous plan of benefit only to the 'Aristocratick Combination'," *Boston Gazette and Country Journal*, November 26, 1787.

2 Quoted in Kyle Scott, *The Federalist Papers: A Reader's Guide* (New York: Bloomsbury Academic Publishing, 2012), 19.

3 Alexander Hamilton et al., *The Federalist Papers*, ed. Isaac Kramnick (Harmondsworth: Penguin, 1987), 25.

4 Hamilton et al., *The Federalist Papers*, 258.

5 Scott, *The Federalist Papers: A Reader's Guide*, 17–33.

6 Hamilton et al., *The Federalist Papers*, 75–6.

MODULE 10
THE EVOLVING DEBATE

KEY POINTS

- *The Federalist Papers* have had a major influence on constitutional law.

- Although no specific school of thought has formed around the work, *The Federalist Papers* have had an important impact on political scientists, legal scholars, judges, and politicians.

- The text has served as a foundation for debates on republicanism,* federalism,* the separation of powers,* and other political issues.

Uses And Problems

Alexander Hamilton, James Madison, and John Jay's *The Federalist Papers* have become a model for understanding the practical institutional principles needed to create and sustain a constitutional* regime. In the discipline of constitutional law, the text defines foundational principles, such as the separation of powers, republicanism, federalism, and constitutionalism itself. It also remains an active part of the debate on the merits of greater political integration (or "union," as its writers called it) versus localism. With the coming of the European Union,* bodies such as the World Trade Organization,* and military organizations such as the North Atlantic Treaty Organization (NATO),* these issues have become central to debates about how political power should be shared between international, national, and local bodies.

This focus on political integration in the text has led to wider debates on the merits of economic integration and freer trade, the

> ❝ *The Federalist* can teach us more about the theory and practice of the Constitution than any other extant work. No other commentary comes close to it in terms of the comprehensiveness and cogency of its defense of America's most fundamental law … Thomas Jefferson famously referred to *The Federalist* as 'the best commentary on the principles of government, which ever was written.[1] ❞
>
> Anthony Peacock, Utah State University

tension between the rights of collective minorities and universal individual rights, and the roles of different branches of government in exercising power and protecting political rights. The authors of *The Federalist Papers* were aware of all of these issues, but they lived at a time when things were simpler in terms of international integration and trade. The debate has far exceeded the bounds of its authors in this respect.

The Federalist Papers are revolutionary and influential for a number of reasons. These include their ongoing usefulness in interpreting the US Constitution; their historical role in helping the constitutional ratification effort; their philosophical and historical content; and the thoroughness with which they link human nature, the political needs of late eighteenth-century America, and universal principles of good government. As George Washington,* the first president of the United States, wrote in a letter to Hamilton, *The Federalist Papers* "will merit the notice of posterity; because in it are candidly and ably discussed the principles of freedom and the topics of government, which will be always interesting to mankind so long as they be connected in civil society."[2]

Schools Of Thought

The Federalist Papers have inspired politicians, judges, scholars, and political philosophers. Notable people in these groups include John

Marshall,* the longest-serving US Supreme Court* Chief Justice; George Washington and Thomas Jefferson,* the first and third American presidents; and William Bennett,* former US secretary of education.[3] Although Washington considered himself a Federalist, both Jefferson and Bennett had views that were not in agreement with the strong-government leanings of Hamilton and the others. But while Jefferson did not agree with the contentions in *The Federalist Papers* regarding term limits and the lack of a Bill of Rights in the Constitution, he nonetheless supported its aims of achieving the US Constitution's ratification and creating a more secure state.

There is no Federalist party in the United States; the ideas contained in *The Federalist Papers* cross both party and ideological boundaries. Parts of the work appeal to political conservatives,* especially those sections that seek to reassure on state power.[4] Other sections will appeal to liberal cosmopolitan thinkers such as David Held,* who emphasizes its arguments about the relationship between human nature and government.[5]

Where regimes in a variety of cultural and political contexts undergo democratization* or other political change, the US Constitution is often used as a starting point and model. John Marshall applied *The Federalist Papers* as a "complete commentary" on the Constitution.[6] Held, on the other hand, has used their philosophical arguments on why government is necessary and how it can best maintain both order and freedom, and extends these to other societies.

In Current Scholarship
References to *The Federalist Papers* today generally come from politicians, judges, political scientists, and legal scholars. They represent the whole spectrum of contemporary political ideologies, legal schools, and judicial approaches. *The Federalist Papers* are cited by conservatives such as Supreme Court Justice Antonin Scalia,* looking to reform the American legal system. They are referenced by liberal

internationalists* such as Held, in supporting universal human rights* and the suitability of democratic government to all humankind. Both possibilities lie within the true spirit of the text.[7] Despite these obvious differences, virtually all followers of the papers believe they provide a model for good governance and the protection of individual freedoms. As such, they are seen as a foundational text for scholars in constitutional law, and as an essential text for scholars of political theory, political economy,* and jurisprudence (legal theory).

Modern disciples of *The Federalist Papers* include influential figures from all branches of the US government and from many of the world's most respected institutions and universities. These people influence legal interpretation, institutional development, and economic prosperity on a global scale, which makes it difficult to imagine a group with more potential to make an impact on the everyday lives of citizens in virtually every part of the world.[8]

NOTES

1 Anthony A. Peacock, "The Federalist Papers," The Heritage Foundation, accessed February 16, 2015, http://www.heritage.org/initiatives/first-principles/primary-sources/the-federalist-papers.

2 George Washington, "Letter to Alexander Hamilton," August 28, 1788, accessed March 16, 2015, http://teachingamericanhistory.org/library/document/letter-to-alexander-hamilton-2.

3 Kyle Scott, *The Federalist Papers: A Reader's Guide* (New York: Bloomsbury Academic Publishing, 2012).

4 See Federalist Nos. 39–46, Alexander Hamilton et al., *The Federalist Papers*, ed. Isaac Kramnick (Harmondsworth: Penguin, 1987).

5 David Held, "Democracy: From City-States to a Cosmopolitan Order?", *Political Studies* 40 (1992): 10–39.

6 Scott, *The Federalist Papers: A Reader's Guide*, x.

7 Hamilton et al., *The Federalist Papers*, 75–82.

8 Scott, *The Federalist Papers: A Reader's Guide*, 173–6.

MODULE 11
IMPACT AND INFLUENCE TODAY

KEY POINTS

- *The Federalist Papers* continue to shape debates on national versus local governments, majority versus minority rights, and the functioning of democratic* institutions.

- One debate in present-day America is over whether the Constitution* should be interpreted in its original form or in its current context.

- The authors acknowledged that the Constitution was a living document that should be amended to suit changing social and political needs.

Position

Alexander Hamilton, James Madison, and John Jay's campaign in favor of the ratification of the Constitution had an enormous impact on American history. It was an experience in which the American people freely debated and chose their form of government. While voting took place at state level, the vote was a national issue of monumental importance, around which a form of national identity emerged.

Today, *The Federalist Papers* have a high-ranking position in American political science. They are recognized as one of the three most important documents in American government and constitutional law, along with the Declaration of Independence* and the Constitution.[2] The US Supreme Court* cited the text in a decision as early as 1798 and has since done so more than 300 times. Its use as a basis for legal opinions has even increased in recent decades.[3]

The Federalist Papers remain at the heart of political debates regarding the roles of national, state, and local governments, the

> **❝[***The Federalist Papers***] are an incomparable exposition of the Constitution, a classic in political science unsurpassed in both breadth and depth by the product of any later American writer. [1] ❞**
>
> Richard Morris, Columbia University, 1987

protection of majority will and minority rights, and the proper roles of various institutions. The authors' ideas regarding human nature, political union, federalism,* and other issues make it relevant beyond the American context.

Interaction

The specific political goal of the authors of *The Federalist Papers* was to ratify the US Constitution. There is, however, evidence they were aware that their work could have long-lasting relevance for the American political system and for principles of government more generally.[4] One of the contemporary debates in which it has played a central role is that between US legal scholars in the "originalist"* school of thought and those who argue for a "living Constitution."* This debate is important in American law because the principle of judicial review says the courts can determine whether or not laws are in accordance with the Constitution. If not, they can be declared unconstitutional and invalidated.[5]

Those who belong to the judicial school of strict constructionism* argue that judges should declare laws invalid if they go beyond explicitly stated powers in the Constitution.[6] This was a key argument made by lawyers and politicians opposed to the 2009 Affordable Care Act ("Obamacare," as it is more commonly called), which was signed into law in 2010. The Act was made law in order to increase the quality and affordability of health care and reduce the number of uninsured people. But a heated debate continues over whether the government has the right to oblige US citizens to buy health insurance. Opponents argue that this directive is not a part of the Constitution and thereby exceeds the power given to Congress.* Supporters argue that the law can be passed under the constitutional authority given to Congress to regulate interstate commerce.[7]

The text can be used by either school of thought. Originalists can use the emphasis of "Federalist No. 42" on the value of political stability and the need for consistent application of the law.[8] In contrast, "living constitutionalists" can appeal to "Federalist No. 84," which notes that the Constitution expressly states that it can be amended to meet future needs.[9]

The Continuing Debate

The Federalist Papers remain an integral part of ongoing debates over the role of government, the specific powers and functions of the American government, and the meaning of the US Constitution. The work is the central focus of debates between strict and "living" constitutionalists. Its role in judicial debates is clear, because it has been cited in over 150 Supreme Court decisions in the past 50 years and it is being cited more often each year.[10] It also features in wider debates on the balance of international, national, and local political power.[11]

The text challenges both the originalist and "living" constitutionalist schools of thought. *The Federalist Papers* clearly argue that consistent interpretation of the Constitution is important for political stability.[12] But it also notes that the Constitution can be changed to suit changing social values and political needs, meaning that its nature as a living document is explicitly acknowledged.[13] It is more challenging to those who argue for rule by a small elite group or to those who claim that democratic government is suited only to local settings and not to larger multicultural states.[14]

The status of *The Federalist Papers* means that few schools or thinkers challenge its legitimacy directly. There are, however, scholars who deny that it should be used in legal interpretation.[15]

NOTES

1   Cited in Duncan Watts, *Dictionary of American Government and Politics* (Edinburgh: University of Edinburgh Press, 2010), 107.

2   See, for example, Michael Meyerson, *Liberty's Blueprint: How Madison and Hamilton Wrote the Federalist Papers, Defined the Constitution, and Made Democracy Safe for the World* (New York: Basic Books, 2008), 135.

3   Meyerson, *Liberty's Blueprint*, 135–6.

4   Alexander Hamilton et al., *The Federalist Papers*, ed. Isaac Kramnick (Harmondsworth: Penguin, 1987), 80–2.

5   Howard Gillman, "The Collapse of Constitutional Originalism and the Rise of the Notion of the 'Living Constitution' in the Course of American State-Building," *Studies in American Political Development* 11, no. 2 (1997): 191–247.

6   Keith Whittington, *Constitutional Interpretation: Textual Meaning, Original Intent, and Judicial Review* (Lawrence: University Press of Kansas, 1999).

7   Mark A. Hall, "Health Care Reform: What Went Wrong on the Way to the Courthouse," *New England Journal of Medicine* 364, no. 4 (2011): 295–7.

8   Hamilton et al., *The Federalist Papers*, 367–9.

9   Hamilton et al., *The Federalist Papers*, 475.

10 Meyerson, *Liberty's Blueprint*, 135.

11 For instance, Bernard Grofman and Donald A. Wittman, *The Federalist Papers and the New Institutionalism*, Series on Representation (New York: Agathon Press, 1989). Also: David Held, "Democracy: From City-States to a Cosmopolitan Order?", *Political Studies* 40 (1992): 10–39.

12 See "Federalist No. 42", Hamilton et al., *The Federalist Papers*, 275–9.

13 See "Federalist No. 84", Hamilton et al., *The Federalist Papers*, 475.

14 Edward Millican, *One United People: The Federalist Papers and the National Idea* (Lexington: University Press of Kentucky, 1990), 119.

15 Meyerson, *Liberty's Blueprint*, 135.

MODULE 12
WHERE NEXT?

KEY POINTS

- *The Federalist Papers* are likely to remain highly influential in the fields of government and jurisprudence (the theory of law).

- It is expected that they will continue to be an important reference point for constitutional law, political theory, judicial theory, and political economy.*

- *The Federalist Papers* are of great historical and rhetorical* interest. They have played a central role in American legal and constitutional interpretation, and in understanding democratization* and human rights.*

Potential

Partly due to the respect given to the authors—Alexander Hamilton, James Madison, and John Jay—and partly because of the dominance of US political norms, *The Federalist Papers* are likely to remain highly influential political and legal texts. Although their applications are sure to stay focused on political philosophy and legal interpretation, these areas must constantly adapt to new realities and new challenges.

The need to respond to new challenges was anticipated by Alexander Hamilton himself, who wrote that he intended the work to "look forward to remote futurity."[2] He hoped it would be of use for a long time to come. As recent scholarly literature shows, *The Federalist Papers* are likely to be increasingly used in debates over privacy in Internet and mobile phone communications.[3] The centrality of US foreign policy in the creation and operation of international institutions, and in humanitarian aid and military intervention globally,

> **❝** It seems that there is no surer way to make clear to others the principles and practices of American government than by rehearsing the very arguments in *The Federalist Papers* ... Coming to understand people who had a clear aim and knew what they were doing gives us the ability to look reflectively upon what we do and what we think. We can, in fact, reconsider some of the assumptions we have held so easily about the practices of American political life. [1] **❞**
>
> W. B. Allen, Professor of Political Philosophy, Michigan State University

means that the work is likely to be used in other political contexts.[4] Debates on globalization,* localism,[5] and the role of American political values in economic institutions might also benefit.[6]

Thousands of court decisions in the United States and thousands of scholarly articles on government, economics, and international relations reference *The Federalist Papers* in order to add authority to their arguments.[7] Their inclusion in political disputes at the international level, and in the new and fast-moving field of Internet privacy, indicates that their power as an interpretive text has grown rather than diminished over time.

Future Directions

The Federalist Papers have influenced a variety of political ideologies, legal schools, and judicial approaches. They have been referenced as a source for interpreting the US Constitution* by conservatives such as Supreme Court* Justice Antonin Scalia,* and have also been cited by liberal internationalists,* such as David Held,* in their scholarship on democracy* and the protection of human rights. While such figures hold contrasting outlooks on government and society, the text is a reference point for both perspectives: for individual freedom and good governance.

The Federalist Papers appear in works on economics and political economy, both of which are used for legal interpretation.[8] Indeed, of the 85 essays, the titles of 10 refer to economics or taxation.[9] Scholars of economics and political economy use the work's positions on taxation and government legitimacy to analyze the extent to which governments are justified in economic interventions.[10]

Another fairly recent development is peer-to-peer (P2P) networks.[11] P2P networks involve two or more computers sharing access to files and external devices without using a server as an intermediary. Publius*—the pseudonym of the writers of *The Federalist Papers*—was the name of one such P2P network launched in the year 2000. The argument is that anonymity is a precondition of free speech in a sensitive or oppressive political context—an extension of the backing of minority rights in *The Federalist Papers*.

The US political system continues to experience tension between defense and individual liberty, between the powers of national and state governments, and between the requirement for increased tax revenue and the need to avoid harming economic growth. All of these issues were present in different forms when the authors wrote their essays.

Summary

The authors of *The Federalist Papers* were all prominent historical figures. James Madison was the fourth president of the United States and drafted much of the US Constitution; Alexander Hamilton and John Jay were the first Treasury* Secretary and the first Supreme Court* justice respectively, and established many of the norms that continue to operate in the management of the Treasury Department and the courts.

The Federalist Papers were a major achievement and expression of cooperative political philosophy at a critical time when a young country was in a state of great uncertainty. Publius wrote 85 essays in less than a year to persuade voters to ratify the new US Constitution, in opposition to the Anti-Federalist* papers, which forcefully sought to preserve the Articles of Confederation.* But Hamilton, Madison, and Jay's views won out and laid the foundation for a political union that has prospered economically and built a formidable military, but which still deals with internal tension.

The Federalist Papers are a cornerstone of American political philosophy and a common reference point in constitutional law. They are relevant to discussions of democratization and human rights, as well as the relationships between national and sub-national governments.[12] In conclusion, it would seem fair to say *The Federalist Papers* will still be providing talking points for another 200 years.

NOTES

1   W. B. Allen and Kevin A. Cloonan, *Federalist Papers: A Commentary—the "Baton Rouge Lectures"* (New York: Peter Lang, 2004), 1–2.

2   Alexander Hamilton et al., *The Federalist Papers*, ed. Isaac Kramnick (Harmondsworth: Penguin, 1987), 81.

3   For example, see Michael Chase et al., "Comrade-to-Comrade Networks: The Social and Political Implications of Peer-to-Peer Networks in China," in *Chinese Cyberspaces: Technological Changes and Political Effects*, ed. Jens Damm and Simona Thomas (London: Routledge, 2006), 57. Also George H. Carr, "Application of US Supreme Court Doctrine to Anonymity in the Networld," *Cleveland State Law Review* 44 (1996): 521.

4   Scholarly works outside the US context include articles such as Deborah J. Yashar, "Democracy, Indigenous Movements, and the Postliberal Challenge in Latin America," *World Politics* 52, no. 1 (1999): 76–104. Also David Held, "Democracy: From City-States to a Cosmopolitan Order?", *Political Studies* 40 (1992): 10–39.

5   Carol M. Rose, "The Ancient Constitution vs. the Federalist Empire: Antifederalism from the Attack on Monarchism to Modern Localism," *Northwestern University Law Review* 84, no. 3 (1989–90): 74.

6   Bernard Grofman and Donald A. Wittman, *The Federalist Papers and the New Institutionalism*, Series on Representation (New York: Agathon Press, 1989).

7   Kyle Scott, *The Federalist Papers: A Reader's Guide* (New York: Bloomsbury Academic, 2012), 173–6.

8   Grofman and Wittman, *The Federalist Papers and the New Institutionalism*.

9   See "Federalist Nos. 11–13, 30–6," Hamilton et al., *The Federalist Papers*.

10 For example, "Federalist Nos. 30–6" all deal with taxation power and are cited by many scholars, including Grofman and Wittman, *The Federalist Papers and the New Institutionalism*. See also Warren Frederick Ilchman and Norman Thomas Uphoff, *The Political Economy of Change* (New Brunswick, NJ: Transaction Publishers, 1998).

11 Articles citing *The Federalist Papers* on Internet anonymity include Chase et al., "Comrade-to-Comrade Networks"; and Carr, "Application of US Supreme Court Doctrine to Anonymity in the Networld," 521.

12 A few examples of these uses include Keith Whittington, *Constitutional Interpretation: Textual Meaning, Original Intent, and Judicial Review* (Lawrence: University Press of Kansas, 1999); Grofman and Wittman, *The Federalist Papers and the New Institutionalism*; Held, "Democracy: From City-States to a Cosmopolitan Order?", 10–39; Michael Meyerson, *Liberty's Blueprint: How Madison and Hamilton Wrote the Federalist Papers, Defined the Constitution, and Made Democracy Safe for the World* (New York: Basic Books, 2008).

GLOSSARY

GLOSSARY OF TERMS

American Revolution/War of Independence: a period from 1775 to 1783 when colonists in the Thirteen Colonies revolted against the British monarchy and founded the United States of America.

Anglican Church: a Christian tradition comprising the Church of England and other churches that share similar beliefs.

Anti-Federalists: a group that opposed the adoption of the new US Constitution and argued that the states should remain firmly in control of political and military power.

Articles of Confederation: document that functioned as the first Constitution of the United States until the ratification of the present Constitution. The Articles aimed to minimize government at the national level and enshrined the local sovereignty of state governments. The Federalists argued that they were too weak and should be replaced by a new Constitution.

Bill of Rights: the first 10 amendments to the Constitution of the United States. The passing of these amendments was due to negotiation with the Anti-Federalists.

Congress: the legislature of the United States located in Washington DC. It is composed of two bodies: the Senate and the House of Representatives.

Constitution: a body of fundamental principles or established precedents according to which a state or other organization is acknowledged to be governed. The Federalists wrote 85 essays in support of a new Constitution as a replacement for the Articles of Confederation.

Constitution of the United States: a document that embodies the fundamental laws and principles by which the United States is governed. It was passed in 1788 and the first 10 amendments, known as the Bill of Rights, were added in 1791. It was later supplemented with other amendments. Publius wrote 85 essays in favor of its passing, in opposition to the Anti-Federalists.

Constitutional Convention: the meeting of state delegates that took place in Philadelphia, Pennsylvania, in 1787 to draft the American Constitution.

Constitutionalism: a political theory whereby every state should be run according to pre-established rules that apply equally to all citizens. Generally, it focuses on limiting state power in areas deemed to be private concerns in order to allow personal liberty.

Declaration of Independence: the document written in 1776 by the American Revolutionaries declaring their intention to create a new state and listing their grievances against the British government.

Democracy: a system of government in which the people exercise power, either directly or through elected representatives.

Democratization: the process by which a state becomes a democracy.

Department of the Treasury: the treasury of the United States government. It was established in 1789 to recommend and formulate economic policies.

Direct democracy: a form of democracy in which people decide policy initiatives directly. The Federalists advocated a system of representative democracy.

Enlightenment: an early modern (seventeenth- and eighteenth-century) cultural, intellectual, and philosophical movement that emphasized social and personal progress through education, science, individualism, and reason. Like Publius, it stressed the importance of republicanism and collective well-being.

European Union: an economic and political union established in 1993 through the Treaty of Maastricht. It built on the European Economic Community, which was established by the Treaty of Rome in 1957. The EU comprises 28 members.

Federalism: a government arrangement in which power is shared between local and national layers of government through defined institutions with clearly specified powers. Publius was in favor of this system of government.

Federalists: a group of politicians who supported the proposed American Constitution between 1787 and 1789, and who advocated for a republic built on the foundations of a strong central government and limited sovereignty for the states composing the federation.

Founding Fathers of the United States of America: the individuals from the 13 North American colonies of Britain who led the Revolution and established the United States of America. The term is also used more narrowly to describe those who either signed the 1776 Declaration of Independence or those who helped draft the Constitution in 1787.

Globalization: the process of becoming global, especially in reference to business and other organizations operating on an increasingly international scale.

House of Representatives: one of the two houses, together with the US Senate, that makes up the United States Congress.

Human Rights: the basic rights and freedoms to which all people are entitled. These include life, liberty, and the pursuit of happiness, among others.

Jim Crow Laws: a period in American history from the end of Reconstruction until the civil rights movements of the 1950s and 1960s when the state and federal governments put a number of impediments in place to prevent black people from reaching greater equality. This was a time when the federal government reinforced state policies that discriminated against African Americans.

Liberal cosmopolitanism: theory which argues that all societies are suited to democratic governance and that all people are entitled to certain universal human rights. This was part of the view of Publius in *The Federalist Papers*.

Liberal internationalism: a foreign-policy concept that suggests that liberal states should involve themselves in the affairs of other sovereign states to pursue their liberal goals.

Living constitutionalism: a school of thought which argues that the US Constitution was always intended to evolve and to be read in a manner suited to the needs and values of the time. Although *The Federalist Papers* were written in a very specific context, their authors envisioned an enduring legacy on governance and jurisprudence.

Majority rule: the principle that whatever a majority of citizens decide with regard to a political issue should become law. This is typically achieved through voting.

North Atlantic Treaty Organization (NATO): an intergovernmental military alliance based on the North Atlantic Treaty, which was signed on 4 April 1949.

Originalists (or strict constructionists): a legal school that argues for the reading and enforcing of a text, in this case the US Constitution, as closely as possible to the original meaning and intent of those who wrote it.

Political conservatism: an ideology that generally seeks to maintain the existing political order and respect for tradition, and prefers political change to occur gradually rather than suddenly. Political conservatives were skeptical of a new Constitution as a replacement for the Articles of Confederation.

Political economy: the study of how governments and their economies are linked and how they can best be regulated to support stability and growth. In *The Federalist Papers*, Publius argued that a stronger central government would bring about greater economic stability.

Protestantism: a form of Christian faith developed out of the Protestant Reformation of the sixteenth century that had fundamental differences from the Catholic Church.

Representative democracy: a form of government in which citizens, rather than making public decisions directly (which is direct democracy), elect a body of representatives who will then act in their name.

Republic: literally, "a thing of the people"—government that represents the rights and needs of the entire public and is supposed to act on their behalf. Elections are held where the people themselves choose political representatives. Publius was in favor of this system of government.

Rhetorical: having to do with the art of speaking or writing, especially with the objective of persuading others to accept something.

Senate: a legislative chamber that, together with the House of Representatives, makes up the US Congress.

Separation of powers: a political theory that claims that the best way to run a government is to divide the role of making law from the roles of enforcing it and making judgments regarding it. This minimizes conflicts of interest and corruption among government workers. Drawing on the arguments of Montesquieu, Publius advocated the separation of powers.

Separatist movement: this is when one group desires to break away from another.

State sovereignty: the understanding that federal government only has powers that have been given to it by the Constitution and that all remaining powers are to be exercised by the states.

States' rights: the American political idea that the individual states maintain certain political powers that cannot be infringed upon by the national government. This was the view of the Anti-Federalists, who feared that a new Constitution would reduce the power of the states.

Strict constructionism: a requirement for judges to make judgments based only on what is written in a legal text, in this case the Constitution.

Supreme Court: the highest court in the United States; its rulings can be overturned only by itself. Importantly, it serves the role of deciding whether or not new laws are consistent with the US Constitution; that is, "constitutional."

Thirteen Colonies: the colonies that composed the original United States in 1776: Connecticut, Delaware, Georgia, Maryland, Massachusetts, New Hampshire, New Jersey, New York, North Carolina, Pennsylvania, Rhode Island, South Carolina, and Virginia. They revolted against the British monarchy and became part of the United States of America.

Tyranny of the majority: the fear, prevalent in republican discourse since antiquity, that popular democracies can devolve into oppressive political systems akin to authoritarian regimes.

War of 1812: a war between Britain and the United States, fought between 1812 and 1815. It has also been called the second American war of independence.

World Trade Organization (WTO): the only global international organization dealing with the rules of trade between nations.

PEOPLE MENTIONED IN THE TEXT

Douglass Adair (1912–68) was a renowned American historian who deciphered the authorship of each of *The Federalist Papers*. His findings have since been affirmed with further evidence.

Aristotle (384–322 b.c.e.) was an ancient Greek philosopher, and one of the most renowned thinkers of all time. His ideas regarding human nature and political organization partly shaped the views of Publius in *The Federalist Papers*.

William Bennett (b. 1943) is an American conservative politician who served as Secretary of Education from 1985 to 1988. He has highlighted the great value of *The Federalist Papers*.

Marcus Tullius Cicero (106–43 b.c.e.) was a Roman statesman, orator, and political leader famous for the beauty of his Latin prose and well known for his political philosophy in works like *On Duties*, *The Republic*, and *On the Laws*. His ideas influenced the views of Publius in *The Federalist Papers*.

Pamela Corley is an associate professor of political science at Southern Methodist University. She has highlighted the great legal value of *The Federalist Papers*.

David Held (b. 1951) is a professor of politics and international relations at Durham University in the United Kingdom, who argues for stronger international institutions and protections for human rights. He has argued that *The Federalist Papers* are a significant historical document with an enduring legacy.

Patrick Henry (1736–99) was an American attorney and politician from Virginia; he was one of the leaders of the Anti-Federalists.

Thomas Hobbes (1588–1679) was an English philosopher best remembered for his book *Leviathan*, in which he established what is now known as social contract theory. Hobbes championed government, specifically the monarchy, as the supreme defense against the chaotic "state of nature." His ideas may have influenced the view of Publius regarding human nature in *The Federalist Papers*.

Robert Howard is professor of political science at Georgia State University. He has highlighted the continuing legal value of *The Federalist Papers*.

David Hume (1711–76) was a key figure of the Scottish Enlightenment. His main ideas suggested that all things had a physical cause and should be discoverable via empirical, or scientifically provable, methods. His ideas helped form the views of Publius in *The Federalist Papers*.

Thomas Jefferson (1743–1826) was the author of the Declaration of Independence and the third president of the United States. He was responsible not only for shaping the political institutions of the United States, but also for expanding its geographical size. He argued that *The Federalist Papers* were the greatest document ever written on American government.

Immanuel Kant (1724–1804) was a German philosopher. His work discusses how governments should ideally be republics and gives justification for political freedom. His ideas had an influence on the views of Publius in *The Federalist Papers*.

John Locke (1632–1704) was an English political philosopher famous for works such as *Two Treatises of Government*, which set out a variety of positions on religious toleration, the protection of property rights, and the promotion of individual well-being that would be adopted by the founders of America.

Donald Lutz is a professor at the University of Houston and works in the area where political theory and American politics intersect.

John Marshall (1755–1835) was Chief Justice of the US Supreme Court from 1801 to 1835. His opinions form the basis of much of present US jurisprudence, including the principle of judicial review where laws can be declared unconstitutional and invalidated by the courts. He relied heavily on *The Federalist Papers* for his decisions.

George Mason (1725–92) was an American politician and delegate from Virginia to the US Constitutional Convention. He was one of the leaders of the Anti-Federalists.

Charles-Louis de Secondat, Baron de Montesquieu (1689–1755) was a French Enlightenment lawyer and author of *The Spirit of the Laws*, which argued that laws must naturally evolve from societies and reflect the customs and values of those societies. His ideas on the separation of powers partly shaped the view of Publius in *The Federalist Papers*.

David Nixon is an associate professor of political science at Georgia State University. He has highlighted the great legal value of *The Federalist Papers*.

Plutarch (c.e. 45–120) was a Greek philosopher, biographer, and essayist whose work *Parallel Lives* included biographies of famous leaders from both Greece and Rome and was widely read for its descriptions of political and social virtue in action. The ancient Roman figure of *Publius* appears in his work.

Publius was the pseudonym of the authors of *The Federalist Papers*. Publius was profiled in Plutarch's writing as having helped establish the Roman republic by overthrowing Rome's kings, importing democratic laws from Athens, and denying himself wealth that would cause envy.

Antonin Scalia (b. 1936) is a US Supreme Court justice who was appointed by President Ronald Reagan in 1986. He is known as a conservative who holds to a constitutional approach called originalism, or strict constructionism, which argues that judges should interpret the Constitution as written and according to its most explicit meaning, and that they should avoid reading implied powers into it.

Kyle Scott is a lecturer in political science at the University of Houston and author of *The Federalist Papers: A Reader's Guide*.

George Washington (1732–99) was a key military leader of the American Revolutionaries in the US War of Independence and the first president of the United States. He established many precedents, such as serving only two terms and using the title "Mr. President," during his presidency. His ideas helped define the views of Publius in *The Federalist Papers*.

James Wilson (1742–98) was a Scottish-born American Founding Father and legal theorist who helped write the US Constitution and served as one of the original Supreme Court justices.

John Witherspoon (1723–94) was president of the College of New Jersey (now Princeton University) and representative of New Jersey in the Constitutional Convention. He signed the Declaration of Independence. An expert on the Scottish Enlightenment, he was a teacher of James Madison.

WORKS CITED

WORKS CITED

Adair, Douglass. "The Authorship of the Disputed Federalist Papers." *William and Mary Quarterly* 1, no. 2 (1944): 97–122.

"The Tenth Federalist Revisited." *William and Mary Quarterly* 8, no. 1 (1951): 48–67.

Allen, W. B. and Kevin A. Cloonan. *Federalist Papers: A Commentary—The "Baton Rouge Lectures"*. New York: Peter Lang, 2004.

Aristotle. *The Politics*. Translated by Carnes Lord. Chicago: The University of Chicago Press, 1984.

Carr, George H. "Application of US Supreme Court Doctrine to Anonymity in the Networld." *Cleveland State Law Review* 44 (1996): 521–46.

Chase, Michael, James Mulvenon, and Nina Hachigian. "Comrade-to-Comrade Networks: The Social and Political Implications of Peer-to-Peer Networks in China." In *Chinese Cyberspaces: Technological Changes and Political Effects*, edited by Jens Damm and Simona Thomas, 57–89. London: Routledge, 2006.

Chernow, Ron. *Alexander Hamilton*. New York: Penguin, 2004.

Corley, Pamela C., Robert M. Howard, and David C. Nixon. "The Supreme Court and Opinion Content: The Use of the Federalist Papers." *Political Research Quarterly* 58, no. 2 (2005): 329–40.

Donovan, Todd, and Shaun Bowler. "Direct Democracy and Minority Rights: An Extension." *American Journal of Political Science* 42, no. 3 (1998): 1020–4.

"A Federalist" (anonymous), "A dangerous plan of benefit only to the 'Aristocratick Combination'," *Boston Gazette and Country Journal*, November 26, 1787.

Ferguson, E. James. "The Nationalists of 1781–1783 and the Economic Interpretation of the Constitution." *Journal of American History* 56, no. 2 (1969): 241–61.

Gillman, Howard. "The Collapse of Constitutional Originalism and the Rise of the Notion of the 'Living Constitution' in the Course of American State-Building." *Studies in American Political Development* 11, no. 2 (1997): 191–247.

Grofman, Bernard, and Donald A. Wittman. *The Federalist Papers and the New Institutionalism*. Series on Representation. New York: Agathon Press, 1989.

Gummere, Richard M. "The Classical Ancestry of the United States Constitution." *American Quarterly* 14, no. 1 (1962): 3–18.

Hall, Mark A. "Health Care Reform: What Went Wrong on the Way to the Courthouse?" *New England Journal of Medicine* 364, no. 4 (2011): 295–7.

Hamilton, Alexander, James Madison, and John Jay. *The Federalist: With Letters of "Brutus."* Edited by Terence Ball. Cambridge: Cambridge University Press, 2003.

The Federalist Papers. Edited by Isaac Kramnick. Harmondsworth: Penguin, 1987.

The Federalist Papers. Edited by Clinton Rossiter. Harmondsworth: Penguin, 2003.

Held, David. "Democracy: From City-States to a Cosmopolitan Order?", *Political Studies* 40 (1992): 10–39.

Hobbes, Thomas. *Leviathan*. London: Hackett, 1994.

Ilchman, Warren Frederick, and Norman Thomas Uphoff. *The Political Economy of Change*. New Brunswick, NJ: Transaction Publishers, 1998.

Jasinski, James. "Heteroglossia, Polyphony, and the Federalist Papers." *Rhetoric Society Quarterly* 27, no. 1 (1997): 23–46.

Jeffrey, William, Jr. "The Letters of 'Brutus': A Neglected Element in the Ratification Campaign of 1787–88." *University of Cincinnati Law Review* 40 (1971): 643.

Kaplan, Lawrence S. *Alexander Hamilton: Ambivalent Anglophile*. Biographies in American Foreign Policy Series. Wilmington: SR Books, 2002.

Kessler, Charles R. Introduction and notes, in Alexander Hamilton et al., *The Federalist Papers*, ed. Clinton Rossiter (Harmondsworth: Penguin, 2003).

Lutz, Donald. *A Preface to American Political Theory*. Lawrence: University Press of Kansas, 1992.

Malins Rose, Walter. *United States Supreme Court Reports*. Rochester, NY: Lawyers Cooperative Publishing, 1901.

Meyerson, Michael. *Liberty's Blueprint: How Madison and Hamilton Wrote the Federalist Papers, Defined the Constitution, and Made Democracy Safe for the World*. New York: Basic Books, 2008.

Millican, Edward. *One United People: The Federalist Papers and the National Idea*. Lexington: University Press of Kentucky, 1990.

O'Donnell, Guillermo. "Horizontal Accountability in New Democracies." In *The Self-Restraining State: Power and Accountability in New Democracies*, edited by Andreas Schedler, Larry Diamond, and Marc F. Plattner. Boulder, CO: Lynne Rienner Publishers, 1999.

Peacock, Anthony A. "The Federalist Papers," the Heritage Foundation, accessed February 16, 2015, http://www.heritage.org/initiatives/first-principles/primary-sources/the-federalist-papers.

Rose, Carol M. "The Ancient Constitution vs. the Federalist Empire: Anti-Ffederalism from the Attack on Monarchism to Modern Localism." *Northwestern University Law Review* 84, no. 3 (1989–90): 74–105.

Scott, Kyle. *The Federalist Papers: A Reader's Guide.* New York: Bloomsbury Academic Publishing, 2012.

Sheehan, Colleen A. "Madison and the French Enlightenment: The Authority of Public Opinion." *William and Mary Quarterly* 59, no. 4 (2002): 925–56.

Stahr, Walter. *John Jay: Founding Father.* New York and London: Hambledon, 2005.

Storing, Herbert J. *The Complete Anti-Federalist.* Vol. 1. Chicago: The University of Chicago Press, 2008.

Washington, George. "Letter to Alexander Hamilton," August 28, 1788, accessed March 16, 2015, http://teachingamericanhistory.org/library/document/letter-to-alexander-hamilton-2.

Watts, Duncan. *Dictionary of American Government and Politics.* Edinburgh: University of Edinburgh Press, 2010.

Whittington, Keith. *Constitutional Interpretation: Textual Meaning, Original Intent, and Judicial Review.* Lawrence: University Press of Kansas, 1999.

Wood, Gordon S. "Ideology and the Origins of Liberal America." *William and Mary Quarterly* 44, no. 3 (1987): 628–40.

Yashar, Deborah J. "Democracy, Indigenous Movements, and the Postliberal Challenge in Latin America." *World Politics* 52, no. 1 (1999): 76–104.

THE MACAT LIBRARY
BY DISCIPLINE

AFRICANA STUDIES

Chinua Achebe's *An Image of Africa: Racism in Conrad's Heart of Darkness*
W. E. B. Du Bois's *The Souls of Black Folk*
Zora Neale Huston's *Characteristics of Negro Expression*
Martin Luther King Jr's *Why We Can't Wait*
Toni Morrison's *Playing in the Dark: Whiteness in the American Literary Imagination*

ANTHROPOLOGY

Arjun Appadurai's *Modernity at Large: Cultural Dimensions of Globalisation*
Philippe Ariès's *Centuries of Childhood*
Franz Boas's *Race, Language and Culture*
Kim Chan & Renée Mauborgne's *Blue Ocean Strategy*
Jared Diamond's *Guns, Germs & Steel: the Fate of Human Societies*
Jared Diamond's *Collapse: How Societies Choose to Fail or Survive*
E. E. Evans-Pritchard's *Witchcraft, Oracles and Magic Among the Azande*
James Ferguson's *The Anti-Politics Machine*
Clifford Geertz's *The Interpretation of Cultures*
David Graeber's *Debt: the First 5000 Years*
Karen Ho's *Liquidated: An Ethnography of Wall Street*
Geert Hofstede's *Culture's Consequences: Comparing Values, Behaviors, Institutes and Organizations across Nations*
Claude Lévi-Strauss's *Structural Anthropology*
Jay Macleod's *Ain't No Makin' It: Aspirations and Attainment in a Low-Income Neighborhood*
Saba Mahmood's *The Politics of Piety: The Islamic Revival and the Feminist Subject*
Marcel Mauss's *The Gift*

BUSINESS

Jean Lave & Etienne Wenger's *Situated Learning*
Theodore Levitt's *Marketing Myopia*
Burton G. Malkiel's *A Random Walk Down Wall Street*
Douglas McGregor's *The Human Side of Enterprise*
Michael Porter's *Competitive Strategy: Creating and Sustaining Superior Performance*
John Kotter's *Leading Change*
C. K. Prahalad & Gary Hamel's *The Core Competence of the Corporation*

CRIMINOLOGY

Michelle Alexander's *The New Jim Crow: Mass Incarceration in the Age of Colorblindness*
Michael R. Gottfredson & Travis Hirschi's *A General Theory of Crime*
Richard Herrnstein & Charles A. Murray's *The Bell Curve: Intelligence and Class Structure in American Life*
Elizabeth Loftus's *Eyewitness Testimony*
Jay Macleod's *Ain't No Makin' It: Aspirations and Attainment in a Low-Income Neighborhood*
Philip Zimbardo's *The Lucifer Effect*

ECONOMICS

Janet Abu-Lughod's *Before European Hegemony*
Ha-Joon Chang's *Kicking Away the Ladder*
David Brion Davis's *The Problem of Slavery in the Age of Revolution*
Milton Friedman's *The Role of Monetary Policy*
Milton Friedman's *Capitalism and Freedom*
David Graeber's *Debt: the First 5000 Years*
Friedrich Hayek's *The Road to Serfdom*
Karen Ho's *Liquidated: An Ethnography of Wall Street*

John Maynard Keynes's *The General Theory of Employment, Interest and Money*
Charles P. Kindleberger's *Manias, Panics and Crashes*
Robert Lucas's *Why Doesn't Capital Flow from Rich to Poor Countries?*
Burton G. Malkiel's *A Random Walk Down Wall Street*
Thomas Robert Malthus's *An Essay on the Principle of Population*
Karl Marx's *Capital*
Thomas Piketty's *Capital in the Twenty-First Century*
Amartya Sen's *Development as Freedom*
Adam Smith's *The Wealth of Nations*
Nassim Nicholas Taleb's *The Black Swan: The Impact of the Highly Improbable*
Amos Tversky's & Daniel Kahneman's *Judgment under Uncertainty: Heuristics and Biases*
Mahbub Ul Haq's *Reflections on Human Development*
Max Weber's *The Protestant Ethic and the Spirit of Capitalism*

FEMINISM AND GENDER STUDIES

Judith Butler's *Gender Trouble*
Simone De Beauvoir's *The Second Sex*
Michel Foucault's *History of Sexuality*
Betty Friedan's *The Feminine Mystique*
Saba Mahmood's *The Politics of Piety: The Islamic Revival and the Feminist Subject*
Joan Wallach Scott's *Gender and the Politics of History*
Mary Wollstonecraft's *A Vindication of the Rights of Women*
Virginia Woolf's *A Room of One's Own*

GEOGRAPHY

The Brundtland Report's *Our Common Future*
Rachel Carson's *Silent Spring*
Charles Darwin's *On the Origin of Species*
James Ferguson's *The Anti-Politics Machine*
Jane Jacobs's *The Death and Life of Great American Cities*
James Lovelock's *Gaia: A New Look at Life on Earth*
Amartya Sen's *Development as Freedom*
Mathis Wackernagel & William Rees's *Our Ecological Footprint*

HISTORY

Janet Abu-Lughod's *Before European Hegemony*
Benedict Anderson's *Imagined Communities*
Bernard Bailyn's *The Ideological Origins of the American Revolution*
Hanna Batatu's *The Old Social Classes And The Revolutionary Movements Of Iraq*
Christopher Browning's *Ordinary Men: Reserve Police Batallion 101 and the Final Solution in Poland*
Edmund Burke's *Reflections on the Revolution in France*
William Cronon's *Nature's Metropolis: Chicago And The Great West*
Alfred W. Crosby's *The Columbian Exchange*
Hamid Dabashi's *Iran: A People Interrupted*
David Brion Davis's *The Problem of Slavery in the Age of Revolution*
Nathalie Zemon Davis's *The Return of Martin Guerre*
Jared Diamond's *Guns, Germs & Steel: the Fate of Human Societies*
Frank Dikotter's *Mao's Great Famine*
John W Dower's *War Without Mercy: Race And Power In The Pacific War*
W. E. B. Du Bois's *The Souls of Black Folk*
Richard J. Evans's *In Defence of History*
Lucien Febvre's *The Problem of Unbelief in the 16th Century*
Sheila Fitzpatrick's *Everyday Stalinism*

The Macat Library By Discipline

Eric Foner's *Reconstruction: America's Unfinished Revolution, 1863-1877*
Michel Foucault's *Discipline and Punish*
Michel Foucault's *History of Sexuality*
Francis Fukuyama's *The End of History and the Last Man*
John Lewis Gaddis's *We Now Know: Rethinking Cold War History*
Ernest Gellner's *Nations and Nationalism*
Eugene Genovese's *Roll, Jordan, Roll: The World the Slaves Made*
Carlo Ginzburg's *The Night Battles*
Daniel Goldhagen's *Hitler's Willing Executioners*
Jack Goldstone's *Revolution and Rebellion in the Early Modern World*
Antonio Gramsci's *The Prison Notebooks*
Alexander Hamilton, John Jay & James Madison's *The Federalist Papers*
Christopher Hill's *The World Turned Upside Down*
Carole Hillenbrand's *The Crusades: Islamic Perspectives*
Thomas Hobbes's *Leviathan*
Eric Hobsbawm's *The Age Of Revolution*
John A. Hobson's *Imperialism: A Study*
Albert Hourani's *History of the Arab Peoples*
Samuel P. Huntington's *The Clash of Civilizations and the Remaking of World Order*
C. L. R. James's *The Black Jacobins*
Tony Judt's *Postwar: A History of Europe Since 1945*
Ernst Kantorowicz's *The King's Two Bodies: A Study in Medieval Political Theology*
Paul Kennedy's *The Rise and Fall of the Great Powers*
Ian Kershaw's *The "Hitler Myth": Image and Reality in the Third Reich*
John Maynard Keynes's *The General Theory of Employment, Interest and Money*
Charles P. Kindleberger's *Manias, Panics and Crashes*
Martin Luther King Jr's *Why We Can't Wait*
Henry Kissinger's *World Order: Reflections on the Character of Nations and the Course of History*
Thomas Kuhn's *The Structure of Scientific Revolutions*
Georges Lefebvre's *The Coming of the French Revolution*
John Locke's *Two Treatises of Government*
Niccolò Machiavelli's *The Prince*
Thomas Robert Malthus's *An Essay on the Principle of Population*
Mahmood Mamdani's *Citizen and Subject: Contemporary Africa And The Legacy Of Late Colonialism*
Karl Marx's *Capital*
Stanley Milgram's *Obedience to Authority*
John Stuart Mill's *On Liberty*
Thomas Paine's *Common Sense*
Thomas Paine's *Rights of Man*
Geoffrey Parker's *Global Crisis: War, Climate Change and Catastrophe in the Seventeenth Century*
Jonathan Riley-Smith's *The First Crusade and the Idea of Crusading*
Jean-Jacques Rousseau's *The Social Contract*
Joan Wallach Scott's *Gender and the Politics of History*
Theda Skocpol's *States and Social Revolutions*
Adam Smith's *The Wealth of Nations*
Timothy Snyder's *Bloodlands: Europe Between Hitler and Stalin*
Sun Tzu's *The Art of War*
Keith Thomas's *Religion and the Decline of Magic*
Thucydides's *The History of the Peloponnesian War*
Frederick Jackson Turner's *The Significance of the Frontier in American History*
Odd Arne Westad's *The Global Cold War: Third World Interventions And The Making Of Our Times*

LITERATURE

Chinua Achebe's *An Image of Africa: Racism in Conrad's Heart of Darkness*
Roland Barthes's *Mythologies*
Homi K. Bhabha's *The Location of Culture*
Judith Butler's *Gender Trouble*
Simone De Beauvoir's *The Second Sex*
Ferdinand De Saussure's *Course in General Linguistics*
T. S. Eliot's *The Sacred Wood: Essays on Poetry and Criticism*
Zora Neale Huston's *Characteristics of Negro Expression*
Toni Morrison's *Playing in the Dark: Whiteness in the American Literary Imagination*
Edward Said's *Orientalism*
Gayatri Chakravorty Spivak's *Can the Subaltern Speak?*
Mary Wollstonecraft's *A Vindication of the Rights of Women*
Virginia Woolf's *A Room of One's Own*

PHILOSOPHY

Elizabeth Anscombe's *Modern Moral Philosophy*
Hannah Arendt's *The Human Condition*
Aristotle's *Metaphysics*
Aristotle's *Nicomachean Ethics*
Edmund Gettier's *Is Justified True Belief Knowledge?*
Georg Wilhelm Friedrich Hegel's *Phenomenology of Spirit*
David Hume's *Dialogues Concerning Natural Religion*
David Hume's *The Enquiry for Human Understanding*
Immanuel Kant's *Religion within the Boundaries of Mere Reason*
Immanuel Kant's *Critique of Pure Reason*
Søren Kierkegaard's *The Sickness Unto Death*
Søren Kierkegaard's *Fear and Trembling*
C. S. Lewis's *The Abolition of Man*
Alasdair MacIntyre's *After Virtue*
Marcus Aurelius's *Meditations*
Friedrich Nietzsche's *On the Genealogy of Morality*
Friedrich Nietzsche's *Beyond Good and Evil*
Plato's *Republic*
Plato's *Symposium*
Jean-Jacques Rousseau's *The Social Contract*
Gilbert Ryle's *The Concept of Mind*
Baruch Spinoza's *Ethics*
Sun Tzu's *The Art of War*
Ludwig Wittgenstein's *Philosophical Investigations*

POLITICS

Benedict Anderson's *Imagined Communities*
Aristotle's *Politics*
Bernard Bailyn's *The Ideological Origins of the American Revolution*
Edmund Burke's *Reflections on the Revolution in France*
John C. Calhoun's *A Disquisition on Government*
Ha-Joon Chang's *Kicking Away the Ladder*
Hamid Dabashi's *Iran: A People Interrupted*
Hamid Dabashi's *Theology of Discontent: The Ideological Foundation of the Islamic Revolution in Iran*
Robert Dahl's *Democracy and its Critics*
Robert Dahl's *Who Governs?*
David Brion Davis's *The Problem of Slavery in the Age of Revolution*

The Macat Library By Discipline

Alexis De Tocqueville's *Democracy in America*
James Ferguson's *The Anti-Politics Machine*
Frank Dikotter's *Mao's Great Famine*
Sheila Fitzpatrick's *Everyday Stalinism*
Eric Foner's *Reconstruction: America's Unfinished Revolution, 1863-1877*
Milton Friedman's *Capitalism and Freedom*
Francis Fukuyama's *The End of History and the Last Man*
John Lewis Gaddis's *We Now Know: Rethinking Cold War History*
Ernest Gellner's *Nations and Nationalism*
David Graeber's *Debt: the First 5000 Years*
Antonio Gramsci's *The Prison Notebooks*
Alexander Hamilton, John Jay & James Madison's *The Federalist Papers*
Friedrich Hayek's *The Road to Serfdom*
Christopher Hill's *The World Turned Upside Down*
Thomas Hobbes's *Leviathan*
John A. Hobson's *Imperialism: A Study*
Samuel P. Huntington's *The Clash of Civilizations and the Remaking of World Order*
Tony Judt's *Postwar: A History of Europe Since 1945*
David C. Kang's *China Rising: Peace, Power and Order in East Asia*
Paul Kennedy's *The Rise and Fall of Great Powers*
Robert Keohane's *After Hegemony*
Martin Luther King Jr.'s *Why We Can't Wait*
Henry Kissinger's *World Order: Reflections on the Character of Nations and the Course of History*
John Locke's *Two Treatises of Government*
Niccolò Machiavelli's *The Prince*
Thomas Robert Malthus's *An Essay on the Principle of Population*
Mahmood Mamdani's *Citizen and Subject: Contemporary Africa And The Legacy Of Late Colonialism*
Karl Marx's *Capital*
John Stuart Mill's *On Liberty*
John Stuart Mill's *Utilitarianism*
Hans Morgenthau's *Politics Among Nations*
Thomas Paine's *Common Sense*
Thomas Paine's *Rights of Man*
Thomas Piketty's *Capital in the Twenty-First Century*
Robert D. Putman's *Bowling Alone*
John Rawls's *Theory of Justice*
Jean-Jacques Rousseau's *The Social Contract*
Theda Skocpol's *States and Social Revolutions*
Adam Smith's *The Wealth of Nations*
Sun Tzu's *The Art of War*
Henry David Thoreau's *Civil Disobedience*
Thucydides's *The History of the Peloponnesian War*
Kenneth Waltz's *Theory of International Politics*
Max Weber's *Politics as a Vocation*
Odd Arne Westad's *The Global Cold War: Third World Interventions And The Making Of Our Times*

POSTCOLONIAL STUDIES

Roland Barthes's *Mythologies*
Frantz Fanon's *Black Skin, White Masks*
Homi K. Bhabha's *The Location of Culture*
Gustavo Gutiérrez's *A Theology of Liberation*
Edward Said's *Orientalism*
Gayatri Chakravorty Spivak's *Can the Subaltern Speak?*

PSYCHOLOGY

Gordon Allport's *The Nature of Prejudice*
Alan Baddeley & Graham Hitch's *Aggression: A Social Learning Analysis*
Albert Bandura's *Aggression: A Social Learning Analysis*
Leon Festinger's *A Theory of Cognitive Dissonance*
Sigmund Freud's *The Interpretation of Dreams*
Betty Friedan's *The Feminine Mystique*
Michael R. Gottfredson & Travis Hirschi's *A General Theory of Crime*
Eric Hoffer's *The True Believer: Thoughts on the Nature of Mass Movements*
William James's *Principles of Psychology*
Elizabeth Loftus's *Eyewitness Testimony*
A. H. Maslow's *A Theory of Human Motivation*
Stanley Milgram's *Obedience to Authority*
Steven Pinker's *The Better Angels of Our Nature*
Oliver Sacks's *The Man Who Mistook His Wife For a Hat*
Richard Thaler & Cass Sunstein's *Nudge: Improving Decisions About Health, Wealth and Happiness*
Amos Tversky's *Judgment under Uncertainty: Heuristics and Biases*
Philip Zimbardo's *The Lucifer Effect*

SCIENCE

Rachel Carson's *Silent Spring*
William Cronon's *Nature's Metropolis: Chicago And The Great West*
Alfred W. Crosby's *The Columbian Exchange*
Charles Darwin's *On the Origin of Species*
Richard Dawkin's *The Selfish Gene*
Thomas Kuhn's *The Structure of Scientific Revolutions*
Geoffrey Parker's *Global Crisis: War, Climate Change and Catastrophe in the Seventeenth Century*
Mathis Wackernagel & William Rees's *Our Ecological Footprint*

SOCIOLOGY

Michelle Alexander's *The New Jim Crow: Mass Incarceration in the Age of Colorblindness*
Gordon Allport's *The Nature of Prejudice*
Albert Bandura's *Aggression: A Social Learning Analysis*
Hanna Batatu's *The Old Social Classes And The Revolutionary Movements Of Iraq*
Ha-Joon Chang's *Kicking Away the Ladder*
W. E. B. Du Bois's *The Souls of Black Folk*
Émile Durkheim's *On Suicide*
Frantz Fanon's *Black Skin, White Masks*
Frantz Fanon's *The Wretched of the Earth*
Eric Foner's *Reconstruction: America's Unfinished Revolution, 1863-1877*
Eugene Genovese's *Roll, Jordan, Roll: The World the Slaves Made*
Jack Goldstone's *Revolution and Rebellion in the Early Modern World*
Antonio Gramsci's *The Prison Notebooks*
Richard Herrnstein & Charles A Murray's *The Bell Curve: Intelligence and Class Structure in American Life*
Eric Hoffer's *The True Believer: Thoughts on the Nature of Mass Movements*
Jane Jacobs's *The Death and Life of Great American Cities*
Robert Lucas's *Why Doesn't Capital Flow from Rich to Poor Countries?*
Jay Macleod's *Ain't No Makin' It: Aspirations and Attainment in a Low Income Neighborhood*
Elaine May's *Homeward Bound: American Families in the Cold War Era*
Douglas McGregor's *The Human Side of Enterprise*
C. Wright Mills's *The Sociological Imagination*

Thomas Piketty's *Capital in the Twenty-First Century*
Robert D. Putman's *Bowling Alone*
David Riesman's *The Lonely Crowd: A Study of the Changing American Character*
Edward Said's *Orientalism*
Joan Wallach Scott's *Gender and the Politics of History*
Theda Skocpol's *States and Social Revolutions*
Max Weber's *The Protestant Ethic and the Spirit of Capitalism*

THEOLOGY

Augustine's *Confessions*
Benedict's *Rule of St Benedict*
Gustavo Gutiérrez's *A Theology of Liberation*
Carole Hillenbrand's *The Crusades: Islamic Perspectives*
David Hume's *Dialogues Concerning Natural Religion*
Immanuel Kant's *Religion within the Boundaries of Mere Reason*
Ernst Kantorowicz's *The King's Two Bodies: A Study in Medieval Political Theology*
Søren Kierkegaard's *The Sickness Unto Death*
C. S. Lewis's *The Abolition of Man*
Saba Mahmood's *The Politics of Piety: The Islamic Revival and the Feminist Subject*
Baruch Spinoza's *Ethics*
Keith Thomas's *Religion and the Decline of Magic*

COMING SOON

Chris Argyris's *The Individual and the Organisation*
Seyla Benhabib's *The Rights of Others*
Walter Benjamin's *The Work Of Art in the Age of Mechanical Reproduction*
John Berger's *Ways of Seeing*
Pierre Bourdieu's *Outline of a Theory of Practice*
Mary Douglas's *Purity and Danger*
Roland Dworkin's *Taking Rights Seriously*
James G. March's *Exploration and Exploitation in Organisational Learning*
Ikujiro Nonaka's *A Dynamic Theory of Organizational Knowledge Creation*
Griselda Pollock's *Vision and Difference*
Amartya Sen's *Inequality Re-Examined*
Susan Sontag's *On Photography*
Yasser Tabbaa's *The Transformation of Islamic Art*
Ludwig von Mises's *Theory of Money and Credit*